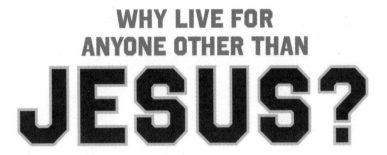

WHY LIVE FOR
ANYONE OTHER THAN
JESUS?

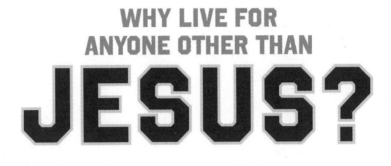

Nathan Stiles

Written By
Donnie Prince

Preface

Oftentimes when we see or read stories about someone in the news, we get a glimpse into a single event of someone's life. But these singular events are not enough information for us to know or understand who that person really was, or the impact their life has had on their friends and family, the people closest to them.

The book you are about to read is a true story about a young man from Spring Hill, Kansas; Nathan Stiles. Nathan was a straight-A student, captain of his Spring Hill High School varsity football team and a member of the varsity basketball team. He was voted Homecoming King of his senior class. Nathan was a member of the Madrigals Vocal program at his school and he sang in his church choir. Nathan was active in his church youth group. He was also a member of a Christian rock band that he and some of his church and high school age friends had formed.

In October of 2010, while playing in a high school football game Nathan collapsed on the sideline. He was life- flighted from the field and in the early morning hours of October 29th, Nathan passed away. Nathan's death quickly became a national news story covered by print and television media outlets around the country.

This book is written to give the reader an insight into the life of Nathan Stiles; what made Nathan the amazing young man he became, and how he developed his strong Christian faith and love of God. How did his family in the midst of their grief after losing Nathan, find the strength to continue to praise God and start a ministry that would touch so many lives, and what can we learn from this inspirational true story?

It has been a blessing to me to get to know his amazing family. I am honored to help them share their story.

Joshua 1:9 New Living Translation (NLT)
"This is my command—be strong and courageous! Do not be afraid or discouraged. For the Lord your God is with you wherever you go."

Foreword

Written By
Natalie Stiles Smith

The most recent affair I had with death was when my brother died. I would like to be able to say it in a more flowery, delicate type of way but when it comes to this, I never know quite how to start. Nathan, that is my brother, was 18 months older than me, but only a grade above me in school. We have been friends since we were little and we were pretty typical siblings in some ways; like in the fighting, tattling, and teasing each other. In other ways though, we were very different. He was one of my best friends, and I mean seriously best friend. Our relationship had become a "let's go on a double date, match on nerd day for spirit week, say "Hi" and hug in the hallway at school every day" type of friendship. More importantly we could talk about anything with each other. One of the most important conversations I had with him was in September after watching "To Save a Life" at the church in town. As we were driving to school the next day we were talking about the movie and how we want to be different. We do not want this passion we have for God to fade this time. We want to live for God in a life changing way and get our classmates in on it too. We were determined that things were going to change for the better.

On October 28, 2010, my brother was playing in the last football game of his senior year in high school. This is the part that is hardest to talk about. There are so many emotions going on, so much happened but I do not know what order, or if the "memories" are really from what other people or the news said that happened, but I'll do my best to remember. My mom saw my brother stumble to the sidelines at halftime. I got a call from a friend on the sideline telling me that my parents should go over there because something was wrong with Nathan. I got a second call soon after saying that my parents REALLY needed to get over there. I don't know what happened after. Someone told me Nathan screamed in pain that his head hurt and then he had a seizure. People kept patting, hugging, watching, and asking what was wrong. Somehow, I ended up on the sidelines with my family. One of the coaches looked like he was doing jumping jacks and kept yelling frantically for help. I am told that the last time my brother moved was when he lifted his hand up towards my mom.

In what seemed to be hundreds of hours later, a helicopter came to take my brother to Kansas University Medical Center, and we raced there by car. The doctors talked to us in a little room and I never knew what they were saying exactly, but it was something like, "we are going to do all that we can but don't get your hopes up." Although I had such a sick, this isn't good feeling, I was sure that my brother would live. My brother cannot die, not yet. Pets die, the old and sick die, but young, God-fearing brothers do not die. Not mine anyway.

I have so many scenes ingrained into my mind that replay over and over again, but when I try to piece it together it is all foggy and a literal blur. My contacts had to be thrown away because they had become so foggy, I am still not sure on the science behind that. Some of the blurs are praying, walking to the waiting room, waiting in the waiting room, praying, people continually showing up to wait in the waiting room, the doctor telling us that they are going to perform surgery on his brain, praying, waiting, more talking, hugging, mostly crying, waiting and praying, doctor talking to mom and dad in the small room again, then, mom screaming. The doctor put an expiration date on my brother of a couple of hours. Nathan was fine that morning and now he is hours from death.

The doctors graciously allowed each visitor to say goodbye to my brother. I will never forget what my brother looked like on that hospital bed. His head was bandaged and he was utterly helpless. The machine that helped him breathe made all of this gross snot stuff come out of his nose; I got to be the one that wiped his nose. What else are best friends for? I held his hand, not the one that had tons of IV tubes in it, the one with the clamp on his finger to read his heart or something. Then he took his final breaths, somebody prayed, and we cried with our whole bodies, more than we ever thought was physically possible. After that we talked with a social worker and all the doctors, and eventually left the hospital. After making a stop at another hospital to tell my grandpa that his grandson died before he found out on the news, we went "home." It really did not feel like home anymore. That feeling that I said could only be described as knowing something was missing was there. Is it possible to call a place home when it feels like that? On November 2, what would be my brother's 18th birthday, we instead held his funeral. He also had a visitation the day before and a celebration of life a couple days after. Now, this is where it gets good. I guess you can say that this is how my family dealt with the grief and try to evaluate it as our family's resiliency or some other textbook definition, but I cannot deny the presence of the Lord I encountered that week. It actually began when we arrived home from the hospital that early morning. We went downstairs to see my brother's Bible on the end table and the imprint in the couch of where he had been sitting there reading it one day earlier. This really put things into perspective for us. So, we believe that there is a Heaven and hell and when we die, we go to one of them. So why am I not living as if that is truly what I believe? Is my life giving people a glimpse of Heaven, or hell?

That night my mom got a vision from God to buy Bibles. So, we brainstormed with local church pastors, friends, and family of how to piece together Nathan's death, our convictions, and this vision. Through these people and pieces, God showed us the Nathan Project. It is not our goal to promote my brother and his life through this, but to proclaim the Good News of Jesus Christ that we, including Nathan, believe and that is why we are able to celebrate his life and death. We want to literally give people the Good News so that they can have a chance to know God for themselves. There were 1,000 Bibles at the celebration of life to give away, and since then there have been over 31,000 Bibles sent to many individuals, multiple states, various groups, and other countries.

Writing this I know I said it was hard to know where to begin, but I am finding it to be even harder to know where to stop. I think that is because it never stops. The hurt never goes away, it just changes and I learn how to deal with it or hide it better. And life never stops, and sometimes that makes the hurting more painful knowing that my life will not consist of any more memories with my brother in it. Nothing will ever be the same. But then again, would I want it to be the same? Isn't that what my brother and I were so passionate about on our car ride that day; to change our lives and lives of those around us for the glory of God? So, while the hurting never stops, the grace and unfailing love never stops either. The revelations and miracles never stop. I could not begin to tell you of all the amazing "coincidences" that have occurred, the friendships formed, family growth, and lives saved as a result of this death.

The last thing I learned about death was that it brings life.

Introduction

"I met him a couple of years ago when I was in the youth detention center," the young man said. "It was a Friday night when they showed up for Bible study, that was the first time I met him. He gave me a Bible and then once me and the other kids took our seats that first night, we read the chapter in Proverbs for that day of the month and discussed what we had read.

"Once I went to the detention center I was forced to slow down and reflect on my life. For the first time I was forced to be away from all the distractions, the cell phone, the drugs. You have to slow down, and you have that Bible with you that he gives away to everyone who asks for one in the center. That Bible was the only possession that I could keep with me all the time, it was the only personal item I could take with me even after I left there, that Bible was mine to keep. I still have that Bible today.

"Every time he came into the center he would ask if anyone needed a Bible, he would give a brand-new Bible still in the plastic wrapper to anyone who wanted one. Even at first, I knew there was something different about this person, but I did not know why he was doing what he was doing, but as I began to read the Bible I would see verses in the Bible that explained to me why he was coming to the center and doing the Bible studies.

"After reading the story in the cover of the Bibles, I thought, '*What does he have in his life that he can do this work after losing his son?*' When I would read my Bible, I came across verses that would remind me of what he was doing, he was living it out. There was one verse in particular that stuck out to me that reminded me of what I saw in him.

John 14:27 "I am leaving you with a gift – peace of mind and heart. And the peace I give is a gift the world cannot give. So, don't be troubled or afraid."

"As I would read this verse, I would immediately think of him, because he has this peace. And I would think, 'That verse is his life.' That is what I saw in him, before I could spiritually verbalize it; I saw that peace in the way he lived.

"I would 100% credit that being able to turn my life around came from having that Bible and the work he is doing. I stayed reading my Bible every day and that changed me. It saved me.

"Now a major goal for me is to find ways to share my experiences with people who are in difficult situations in life; because I have been there myself. I know where those roads lead. I was in that spot; I know how deceiving that lifestyle is. But I can honestly say to someone with a 100% truthful heart; that no matter where you are in life, that there is a silver lining in the clouds, when we turn to Jesus and He begins to pull you out of that lifestyle, from the depths of despair, that with Jesus, there is always hope."

Part 1

1

If you were to make a short list of the best places to raise a family in America, you would place Spring Hill, Kansas near the top of the list.

Spring Hill is a small town with a population of just over 6900 people, where quiet neighborhoods and a well-kept historic downtown district are surrounded by scenic rural farms of row crops and livestock that line the gently rolling east Kansas landscape. Spring Hill offers the peace and quiet of a small-town Midwestern community, while being only a 10-minute commute west to the larger city of Olathe, Kansas with its population of 139,000, and a 45-minute drive north up I-35 to Kansas City.

In addition to its deeply rooted history of agriculture, Spring Hill is now considered a part of the Kansas City metropolitan area, making Spring Hill a popular real estate destination for families who want to raise their children in a small community where neighbors know each other by name, and yet have easy commutes to the larger communities of Olathe and Kansas City.

A lot has changed in Spring Hill over the years as the Kansas City metro area has grown to encompass Olathe and Spring Hill, but one thing that has not changed, is the small-town farming community values of faith, family and fellowship that make Spring Hill such a special place to live.

Ron Stiles grew up on a farm in Spring Hill, Kansas. And many of the life lessons he learned as a kid growing up and working around the farm, have had a positive influence on him throughout his life.

"I was very blessed growing up on a farm and having a dad that was blessed with wisdom," Ron recalls, "which is something I wish I would have better understood at the time. He was always teaching me a valuable lesson in a humble way, so that I could learn on my own while he kept watch over me."

The Stiles family always had a garden that Ron says was a very necessary part of the farm. Ron remembers that taking care of the family garden was a lot of work. It was working in the family garden where Ron's dad, Robert Stiles, came up with a plan to teach Ron a lesson about the value of money, and the importance of making his own way in the world.

During the fall of the year when it was time for the Miami County Fair to be held in nearby Paola, Kansas, the family farm's potato crop would be ready for harvest. Ron says it would take a lot of buckets being filled with potatoes by hand to harvest all those potatoes. So, Robert Stiles came up with a plan for Ron to participate in the harvesting, allowing Ron to make some money to spend at the fair. Ron would help harvest the potatoes and be paid for gathering the potatoes into buckets. For every small bucket Ron would earn a dime, and every large bucket a quarter. This would give Ron the money he would need as a small boy, to pay for the things he wanted at the fair. He had to work for it, and that way of thinking would continue to guide Ron throughout the rest of his life.

As Ron grew to be a little older, his dad gave him additional responsibility. Ron recalls one year when Robert Stiles put Ron in charge of two pigs that he was to feed and take care of, and later those pigs would be taken to the fair where they would be sold. Ron would then get the money from the sale of the two pigs to use as his spending money for the rest of the year.

The two pigs were being kept in a barn with an outside run area that had a door that led into a barn that would protect the pigs from the sun. One day, Ron's dad told him he needed to secure, nail, that gate door open, so the pigs would not accidently push the door shut and be stuck out in the hot sunlight where they might die. Ron ignored that instruction. Later one hot afternoon, he found that the pigs had done just that. The pigs had pushed the door shut and been trapped outside in the summer sun. Ron's pigs had died. Not only did he feel terrible about the pigs dying while in his care, but in addition to that, Ron says, that when the pigs died, his whole net worth had vanished.

Later that very night, Ron overheard his mom asking his dad if he was going to give Ron some of the other pigs on the farm to take care of until it was time for the county fair. Ron remembers that his dad had over 100 other pigs on the farm at the time. Ron felt a glimmer of hope until he heard his dad tell his mom, "I told him to secure that door open."

Ron did not receive any of his father's pigs. That was an important lesson for Ron, his dad was teaching him how to work his own way out of his own mistakes.

Years later when Ron was in high school there was one evening in particular when he had not been so good, as he recalled he had, "caused some problems at home." Later that same evening after dinner, there was a load of shelled corn that needed to be scooped into a bin at the barn. This was a task that Ron and his dad would usually do together and would go fairly quickly. That evening though there was only one shovel in the trailer as Ron and his dad backed the pickup truck into the barn. Ron's dad told him to unload the load of corn by himself. To Ron it looked like a mountain that would take forever. So, Ron asked his dad how he could ever get all of this corn unloaded. His dad's response was, "one scoop at a time."

"Many times, in my life I have seen mountains before me, and that advice from my dad has helped me ever since," Ron remembers. "I have shared these stories many times with the youth I work with today, trying to pass on some of the valuable lessons Dad blessed me with while I was growing up on the farm."

Robert Stiles

2

It was the summer of 1978, and Ron was 23 years old, when the opportunity came along for him to purchase the Spring Hill Oil Company which was located in the historic downtown area of Spring Hill. Purchasing the oil company would be one of the keys to opening the door to future opportunities for Ron to grow as a businessman and develop personal contacts in the Spring Hill community as it continued to grow and prosper. The oil company was an existing business at the time Ron bought it, but as is the case with any business venture there were lots of challenges. As the years passed, Ron continued to operate the oil company and make his home in the Spring Hill area.

Ron would later become one of the original board members of the Spring Hill Chamber of Commerce, and he served two years on the Spring Hill City Council from 1998 to 2000. Ron would also later serve fourteen years as a Miami County Commissioner.

November 20, 1987, Ron married Connie Morrison, and along with Ron's three children from a previous marriage, a daughter Josie, and two sons Nick and Clinton, the five of them began their new lives together. Connie Stiles also grew up on a farm in Spring Hill where her parents, Eldon and Judy Morrison, owned a dairy farm.

Nathan was born on November 2, 1992 and then when his younger sister Natalie came into the world on May 13, 1994, the Stiles family was complete.

One of the main priorities from the beginning in the Stiles household was church. Ron's parents, Robert and Catherine Stiles, and Connie's parents, Eldon and Judy Morrison, had also made church a priority in their homes. That model of family and faith was something that Ron and Connie committed to early on in their marriage and they eagerly supported all of their children in their faith journeys.

Ron's mother directed the choir in the First Methodist Church in Spring Hill where she played the piano and organ. Connie's parents also attended Spring Hill Methodist. Over the years Eldon sang for many funerals and other occasions in and around the Spring Hill community. Their love of music was shared by Connie, who is gifted with an angelic singing voice. She often played the piano at home, singing with the children, helping them develop their musical gifts. Connie also later played the piano and directed the choir at church.

Labor Day weekend 1997, Ron had been at a lake outing with some friends when he noticed a strange feeling in his side. At first, he did not think much about it. Like most men, Ron did not want to go to the doctor unless it was absolutely necessary, so he just lived with the discomfort for the next two weeks hoping whatever was wrong would heal. A few days later while playing a round of golf, and again in the following days at a Kansas City Chiefs' football game, he began to run a high fever and the pain resurfaced, he knew it was time to go to the doctor and get checked out.

"Since I hated going to the doctor, for some strange reason I decided to go to a small-town doctor. Looking back on it now, that seems like a strange decision," Ron recalled as he told the story, "since this doctor was in a clinic 20 miles away in Osawatomie, Kansas, I had to drive from Spring Hill, and then on past Paola, Kansas, where there were several doctors."

It was in this clinic in Osawatomie, Kansas, where Ron would meet Dr. Jeff Dorsett. Dr. Dorsett examined him and suspected that Ron may have a ruptured appendix. Dr. Dorsett referred him to a nearby clinic in Paola, Kansas, a few miles down the road to have a scan of his appendix where it was determined his appendix had indeed ruptured. Ron was soon admitted to the hospital in nearby Olathe, about 10 miles from his home in Spring Hill, Kansas, where he had his appendix removed.

Ron spent the next week in the hospital following surgery.

"That week in the hospital was a very tough week", Ron remembers. "I ran a high fever and was in a lot of pain. It was a wakeup call that I was not going to live forever, and although I believed in Jesus, my walk with him was not good."

Over the years there had been times when Ron would be in a group of people talking about the Bible, and others in the group would give their opinions about what the scripture says as they discussed passages. As Ron recovered from his appendix scare, he decided it was time for him to read the Bible for himself, so he began to read the Bible from cover to cover. It took a year.

"Little did I know it was going to start changing me, little by little.

"After some resistance on my part, I started to be a part of a Sunday school class trying to learn more about God's Word. I did not realize how much reading the Bible was changing me until years later. What always stuck out to me as I read the Bible that year, is that many of the mistakes I made earlier in my life probably would not have happened if I had read the Bible when I was younger."

Over the next two years church became a bigger part of Ron's life, helping him grow in a lot of ways. Just as Ron was becoming more and more excited about his new walk with Jesus, a change came within the church. There was a change in pastoral leadership that would become very frustrating to him as time went on, yet Ron and his family continued to be involved in the church.

Then one day while helping with the church's summer Vacation Bible School program, Ron was helping serve juice and milk to the children when all at once a thought came to him, "It's okay to leave." Ron says his eyes felt as though someone had taken a picture and the light from the flash bulb had impaired them. He knew just what it meant. It was okay to leave the church. This was not going to be easy however; Ron and Connie's families were long time members of this church, and Nathan and Natalie were young at the time. At first this thought of leaving the church they had attended for so many years was very disturbing to both Ron and Connie. For the next few days Ron read through his Bible gleaning for information, hoping some verses would jump out at him telling him more, but it didn't.

Ron says he felt like God was telling him it was okay to leave, but that he did not have to go, or if they left, where they should go. That following Sunday Ron played golf and at that golf outing a friend told Ron about Pastor Kirk Johnston and his church in Paola, Kansas. The Stiles family ended up going to this church for almost three years. For some strange reason Ron says when they drove to their new church that first Sunday in Paola, they drove past Hillsdale Presbyterian Church and said, 'we could go there.' After several years, the family made the move to change churches again and go to Hillsdale, where Pastor Kirk Johnston's wife, Laurie Johnston, was the pastor. As the years passed Hillsdale Presbyterian Church would become a very important part of the Stiles' faith journey.

The Stiles quickly became a part of the Sunday school program at Hillsdale. Before long Nathan and Natalie were doing their own little church service at their grandma's house on Sundays.

"Hillsdale Presbyterian Church turned out to be the perfect fit for us," Ron said. "Nathan and Natalie were very involved in the Hillsdale Sunday school program. They were blessed to have some very special Sunday school teachers who poured themselves into Nathan and Natalie and the other children who attended Hillsdale."

Mary Goetz taught Sunday school at Hillsdale for years, working with the younger children. Mary taught the children stories from the Bible and the value of memorizing scripture. One year, Mary decided to initiate a program to encourage the children in her class to memorize all the names of the books of the Bible in order, both the Old and the New Testaments. Mary decided to offer a leather-bound study Bible as an incentive to any child who memorized all the names of the Bible books. Nathan was the first one of his group to memorize all of the Bible books and receive a leather-bound study Bible with his name engraved on the front cover. Natalie would soon follow.

As the children got older, they advanced into the upper level children's program at Hillsdale, taught by Loree Hieber. Loree noticed early on that Nathan had the unique ability to sense what other people were feeling.

"Nathan was an unusually gifted child. There was nothing that Nathan could not do and do well." Loree continues, "Sports, school work, music, anything he wanted to do he could do it. And he had this ability to make everyone comfortable around him no matter their age. Even as a child, Nathan was somehow able to sense what other people were feeling and needing, and he was able to give them the emotional support they needed. He was especially attentive to his sister Natalie and his mother Connie; they were very close. He was very mature and sensitive for his age. He had the ability to make everyone feel special, to make you know that he cared about you, that you were his friend. He was always trying to find ways to be kind to other people."

One year while Nathan was in high school Loree gave every student in her Sunday school classes a study Bible. Inside each study Bible was a daily reading devotional of an Old Testament passage, a New Testament passage, a Psalm and a Proverb, that if followed daily each student would read through the entire Bible in one year. Once Nathan received his study Bible, he took the challenge to read through the Bible very seriously. Loree says he worked on it faithfully. Reading through the Bible that year would have a very powerful effect on Nathan. Just as reading the Bible had impacted his father Ron.

Nathan would later go on to post on his social media page, "Why Live for Anyone Other Than Jesus?"

One day during the Sunday morning church service Loree was sitting next to Nathan when the time came for the congregation to stand and sing. When the music began and Nathan began to sing and Loree heard his voice she immediately thought, '*Nathan needs to be in the choir.*' At that time there were only adults singing in the Hillsdale Church choir. Connie was the choir director and Ron was singing in the choir. After the church service ended Loree went up to Pastor Laurie and Connie and told them, "Nathan has this amazing voice and he needs to be singing in the choir."

Not long after that Nathan joined the adult choir group. Once that happened and his grandfather Eldon found out Nathan was singing in the choir, Eldon on occasion would come over to Hillsdale on Sunday mornings where he would sing in the choir with Ron and Nathan, while Connie played the piano.

3

When the Stiles children were small, they spent a lot of time with their grandparents on their family farms. Nathan and Natalie, like their older brothers Nick and Clinton, and their sister Josie, all loved to be outdoors on the farm. Oftentimes, their grandfathers, Eldon and Robert, would take the kids walking on the farms and out to the livestock shows, where the kids would get ice cream and go for rides on pickup trucks and sit atop farm equipment, spending time together.

Eldon recalls one time in particular when he had taken Nathan out on the farm with him riding in his truck. As Eldon and Nathan drove along together, they came upon a fence with a gate that needed to be opened so they could pass by.

Eldon put the truck in neutral and left the engine running as he got out of the pickup truck to open the gate, leaving Nathan alone in the cab passenger seat. When Eldon got out in front of the vehicle to open the gate, as he was standing directly in front of the truck, he heard the engine rev up and Eldon says, "It scared me half to death thinking I was going to be run over."

Eldon quickly turned around and looked back through the windshield glass for Nathan, but he could not see him because Nathan was so short that his head was lower than the dashboard. Nathan had climbed down from the passenger seat and was standing on the floor board of the truck, with his hands holding tightly on the steering wheel, his foot on the gas pedal as he continued to rev up the truck's engine. Eldon quickly made his way back around to the driver's door, where he saw Nathan standing there with a surprised look on his face. "Nathan, you scared me half to death!" said Eldon. Nathan replied, "That scared me too, Grandpa!"

Nathan, like most little boys, had tons of energy, and there were times when his boundless energy and curiosity would get the best of Connie. Like many little boys Nathan was especially close to his mother. He was into everything, and like all children, he desired attention, especially from his mom.

Connie remembers one time in particular, when Nathan was going through a period where he thought he was a superhero and was convinced he could fly. So, Nathan found himself some sort of fabric material and wrapped it around himself like a cape, and proceeded to go out into the backyard and start jumping off the slide on the swing set like Superman, determined he would fly.

After a few attempts at air flight Nathan crashed into the ground, much to his disdain, and injured his leg which required a trip to the pediatrician for examination. On the ride to the doctor's office Connie gave Nathan a stern talking to about the dangers of jumping from the top of the jungle gym set while attempting to fly, trying to convince Nathan that it was impossible for little boys to fly like Superman.

Once Connie and Nathan got in to see the doctor, Connie asked Nathan's pediatrician to explain to Nathan that it was not possible for children to fly. So, the doctor did as Connie asked, and painstakingly explained to Nathan that flying was not a possibility for him, and he needed to give up hope that if he jumped off the swing set, even with a cape on, he would be able to fly.

Later after the doctor's visit on the drive home, Connie remembers Nathan still unconvinced saying, "That doctor doesn't know me, I can fly."

4

Dana Broockerd and Connie Stiles have been friends for years. The two women went to Spring Hill High School together and were both part of the cheerleading squad. After high school, Dana Broockerd opened a daycare, that she still operates today in the community of Spring Hill.

When Nathan was about three or four years old, he and Natalie began to go to Dana's daycare that she operated at that time in her home. It was there that Dana's son, Cole, and Nathan became friends, and the boys would remain close friends throughout high school.

"I love that family," says Cole, as he reminisced about his time growing up with Nathan, Natalie and the rest of the Stiles family.

"My mom and Connie went to high school together. My mom has had a daycare for years now. When I was small, she had the daycare in our home. Now she has a daycare facility located at a different location in town with over 100 kids in it. Nathan started coming to daycare at our house when we were three or four years old and Natalie, who was a year or so younger than Nathan, came too. Nathan and I knew each other from the time we were small kids, and were friends all through school.

"As we grew older, we would play airsoft and video games. In the summer Ron and Connie were working, so Nathan and Natalie would come over and stay at our house where we spent all of our summer days together. They had a pool at Nathan's house and we would go over there and play sometimes, too. We played baseball together and various other sports. In the summer we would play in baseball tournaments and sometimes that meant we would go out of town and stay with host families in their homes. We spent a lot of time together.

"Once we reached fourth or fifth grade we began to stay over at friend's houses and at that point I began to go with Nathan to church some. If you were going to spend Saturday night over at Nathan's house, that meant that you would be going to church on Sunday morning."

Cole and Nathan shared many childhood experiences together, birthday parties, pool parties, little league sports. Cole remembers there was one night in particular when Cole invited Nathan and some of his other friends to spend the night at his house for a sleepover/birthday party when things got pretty intense.

"I remember there was one year, maybe I was four or five years old and I had a birthday party over at my house, and Nathan and some other boys slept over that night. Since it was my birthday my mom let us stay up late, so they were asleep before we went to bed. Sometime during the night while everyone else was asleep, Nathan called Connie to come and get him and she asked him if he had told anyone he was leaving and he said, 'Yes.' The next morning when I woke up, we looked around and Nathan was gone. We looked for him but when we could not find him, we told my mom and she was beginning to worry that she had lost Nathan. Finally, after looking for him a while, she called Connie to tell her Nathan had gone missing. That's when Connie told my mom that Nathan had called earlier that morning and they had come and picked him up. Connie got on Nathan pretty good for that. We were always doing things together when we were younger. I have really good memories of my time spent with Nathan and his family."

As anyone who has been blessed to have a close relationship that begins as a small child and carries on with someone through their formative years can relate to, Cole and Nathan's friendship was very special.

When the boys grew older and they were given more freedom to play on their own the complexity and number of participants in their games grew.

Cole says it was around the fifth grade that the boys discovered airsoft pellet guns. Soon after that they began to organize airsoft battles with other kids at Cole's house. As they got older, more and more kids became involved in these airsoft battles as the popularity of airsoft grew. Cole says once they were old enough to drive, they would go over to one of Nathan's grandfather's farms and they would have 15 or 20 kids playing. "Those airsoft battles were intense. Most days each of the kids playing would shoot off thousands of pellets a piece. Nathan and I played airsoft at least once a week or so for seven or eight years," said Cole.

"We still have millions of those airsoft pellets in our backyard." Cole continues, "I remember a year or so ago we were digging a hole for a post in the backyard at my parents' house, and when we dug the hole for the post the soil was filled full of airsoft pellets from those games we played when we were kids ten or fifteen years ago."

Another time when Cole and Nathan were older, the two boys went to the fireworks stands in town around the fourth of July and bought up a bunch of fireworks. The two of them bought some ten shot Roman candles, and brought them back to Nathan's house. Cole says it was probably about ten o'clock at night when Cole and Nathan went out into Nathan's backyard to shoot off the fireworks. Meanwhile, Ron was inside trying to sleep because he had somewhere he needed to be early the next day. Nathan and Cole took the fireworks out in the back yard and proceeded to light them.

"We had no idea how loud those things were going to be. We set the first one off and that thing was so loud! Ron came out the back door and we were just standing there as the rest of them started to go off. Ron was not happy. There were ten of those things and once they were lit there was no way to stop the rest of them from firing. We got into some trouble over that, too."

Later, as the boys grew older and went on to high school there was an event that Cole said best explained what type of person Nathan was, and what their friendship was like.

"During February of my junior year I had surgery, and the wound did not heal properly. Over the next several months I had to have another surgery and then some other procedures while the wound was healing. During that time, I was not able to get out and do things like normal and I was at home alone a lot. That was a dark time for me, having to go through that, and me not being as active as I would have liked while waiting for the wound to heal. Nathan made a point during that time to come and visit me on a regular basis. A lot of that time was in the summer when he could have found other things to do instead of coming to visit me. But he came to see me regularly during that time. Nathan showed me what it meant to be a friend.

"That was a really hard time for me, being at home alone so much with my health issues. Nathan's coming to visit with me consistently during that time meant a lot to me. The next year when I went off to school, I was not sure what I wanted to do. I did know that I wanted to do some type of job where I would be able to help people and see that what I was doing was making an impact on people's lives. Looking back on it now, I think my experiences with Nathan influenced my decision to go into a field where I make a difference helping others.

"Nathan was always kind to everyone. Our friendship and the time we spent together helped solidify my decision to become a firefighter-paramedic."

5

It was a cool rainy day in May near the end of the school year. Ron and Connie were in Mound City, Kansas where Nathan was scheduled to run a 100-meter preliminary race in a middle school regional track meet. Nathan was in the seventh-grade at the time and he had run very well all year during the middle school track season, as well as excelling in football and basketball on the Spring Hill Middle School teams. Natalie, who was eighteen months younger than Nathan but only one grade behind him in school, also excelled in athletics, playing basketball and running track on the Spring Hill Middle School teams.

As the day progressed, the weather conditions continued to deteriorate. Meanwhile, Ron and Connie were stuck out in the miserably cold, rainy weather where they sat anxiously awaiting the time for Nathan's race to be contested. Finally, the time came for Nathan's race. His name was called over the track's loud speaker system, notifying him to report to the starting line and move into the runner's blocks to begin the race. The gun went off to begin the race and as the runners raced down the track, Nathan's lane was empty. Ron and Connie later found out Nathan was eating a hamburger in the hospitality tent when his race was announced and he had not heard his name called. Needless to say, Ron and Connie were wet, cold and not happy.

Shortly after Nathan missed his start time the meet was halted and postponed due to rain, it was rescheduled to be finished the next week in Wellsville, Kansas.

With Nathan missing his preliminary heat he was not eligible to participate in the 100-meter final. Since athletes could participate in three meet events, him missing the qualifying for the 100-meter opened up a spot for Nathan to be added into another meet event. So, the coaches added Nathan as a member of the relay team. Initially, Ron was disappointed, because the 100-meter had been Nathan's most successful event all season and he wanted to see how Nathan would have done in the 100-meter final against the region's fastest runners.

When the time came for the relay event, Nathan was scheduled to run the final leg of the relay. The gun went off and from the outset the Spring Hill boys were running their hearts out trying to stay in the race. Ron was sitting there in the stands and his heart began to sink still thinking about how Nathan had missed the 100-meter finals, as he watched the relay team drifting further back from the lead runners. The other boys on the Spring Hill team had run as hard as they could, but when Nathan was handed the baton, the Spring Hill boys were close to, if not, in last place.

As Ron looked out over the track, he saw Nathan rounding the first corner and he was quickly gaining ground on the other runners. Suddenly, Ron says he forgot about the missed 100-meter finals as Nathan continued to gain ground on the rest of the field. When Nathan reached the finish line, he had passed most of the runners in the field and moved the team into third place where all the relay team would receive a medal. Nathan was thrilled. He and all of his buddies on the relay team were jumping up and down in celebration. Ron says that Nathan always cherished doing anything with his buddies.

"As a father," Ron exclaimed, "I was most proud of Nathan for the way he always thought of others before himself. That's a lesson, as his dad, I needed to get better at. Today, I often think of that empty lane, and how it turned out with Nathan and his friends celebrating their third-place finish together at the end of that race, and how he was always thinking of others and doing his best. We all need to give it all we have and finish the race; the race Paul talks about in 2 Timothy 4:7 - *"I have fought the good fight. I have finished the race, and I have remained faithful."* (NLT) Still today all these years later I am trying to do just that."

6

Eric Kahn knew Nathan from the time they were in grade school. The boys did not go to the same elementary school but they did play youth sports together in the Spring Hill recreation leagues. Once the boys moved into middle school, they started playing basketball on the Spring Hill Middle School team together and it was at that point their friendship began to grow. Then, as Eric and Nathan moved on through middle school and then into their high school years the boys' friendship continued to develop.

Eric says that when the boys weren't playing sports, they often would play video games, and sometimes would go hit golf balls together. Eric remembers that one of their favorite things to do was play airsoft. Whenever they got the chance they would hook up with Cole and get a group up of some of their other buddies and meet at Nathan's grandfather's farm and play airsoft pellet war games. There, down in this valley formed by two large hills, with woods on each side, the boys would divide up into two teams of 10 people each and have day long airsoft pellet battles which at times would become quite intense.

"Nathan was always very intense about those airsoft games. He had some spunk about him," Eric said. "Nathan was a very competitive person."

As they got older Eric excelled in soccer as a standout player on the Spring Hill varsity soccer team. Then one day, before the start of his junior year, one of the football coaches

21

approached Eric about kicking for the Spring Hill football team. High school football and soccer are both played in the fall in Kansas, so Eric knew that playing two sports in one season could cause a problem if both the soccer team and football team happen to have a game scheduled on the same day.

Eric talked with his high school soccer coach about it and his soccer coach agreed to let Eric kick for the football team, as long as if there ever were to come a day when the football and soccer teams were playing games at the same time, Eric would play for the Spring Hill soccer team instead of playing in the football game. This scheduling conflict would become an issue for Eric only once during his high school career. The night of October 28th, 2010, the Spring Hill soccer team would play a state playoff soccer game, while the Spring Hill football team played their last game of the football season in Osawatomie, Kansas. It was the only high school football game Eric was not able to participate in due to him playing soccer.

Both of the boys, Nathan and Eric, excelled athletically and also in the classroom, they had a lot in common. Eric says that during their high school years they became very close friends. When Eric recalls the time he spent with Nathan, what Eric remembers most about Nathan was the way he treated people.

"Nathan was a very kind human being," Eric said as he reflected about his friendship with Nathan. "He was one of our top athletes in school, but he never thought of himself as being above anyone else. He had a touch of God about him in the way he carried himself and the way he treated other people. He would go out of his way to be inclusive of everyone, to make kids who may not have been a star athlete on the basketball team or a 4.0 student in the classroom feel that he cared about them. Not all of us in school were as involved in our faith as Nathan was. He had a sense of morals that rubbed off on us. He never forced his ideas about faith on anyone. It was the way he lived out his faith. Looking back on it now I can see that I learned a lot from Nathan.

"When we were together, we would often talk about something that was happening in school or a situation about something we would see, and then we would discuss what was happening from a faith perspective. Nathan was always willing to discuss faith issues; sharing his faith when the opportunity presented itself was not something he would shy away from.

"Watching the way Nathan treated everyone with respect and kindness, treating everyone equally, observing him do that helped me to see that that was important. I know now the impact you leave on people is what is important, that is what I learned the most from the time we spent together as friends. Nathan was popular, a 4.0 student, a varsity athlete, but he treated everyone the same way. He didn't partake in alcohol or some of the other things that kids in school were tempted to do, he was very comfortable in his values. And yet, he did not judge anyone for what they might be doing. He found a way to fit in and be a part of the group, while maintaining his own moral standards.

"Church was always important to Nathan and his family. You could see that church had a positive influence on who Nathan was as a person. Whenever I would be over spending the night at Nathan's house and Sunday morning would roll around, he and his family would be up early getting ready for church."

From a teammate's perspective in athletics, Eric remembers that Nathan had a work ethic that was second to none. He stated that Nathan was self-motivated, and he maintained a 100% positive attitude. Nathan worked diligently to be the best player he could be for himself and his team.

"Some of the most special times I remember spending with Nathan, was when sports practice would end for the day, and after practice we would leave from practice together and drive over and get something to eat just the two of us, those times when we would have one-on-one time together and talk."

Eric Kahn and Natalie Stiles

7

During Nathan's freshman year of high school, the school counselors at Spring Hill were looking for some young men from the student body to become involved in their Peer Helpers program. Peer Helpers is a mentoring program where students are nominated to attend a leadership training retreat. At the retreat the students are taught peer-helping skills, where they are instructed on how to have meaningful conversations with their peers about everyday issues that teens often face.

In addition, as part of the retreat the student participants learned how to better manage their own problems and to be sensitive to the issues, they and their classmates are facing that may be too big to face alone. They were taught these skills with the idea that they might be able to help other students in need of someone to talk with when a difficult situation with a fellow student might arise. After the retreat once the school year started, the Peer Helpers students were simply encouraged to be present for their friends, to listen and support their student peer group through some of the challenging situations teenagers often face while in high school.

Katie George, a counselor at Spring Hill High School, was the sponsor of the Peer Helpers program while Nathan was a student at Spring Hill.

"The year Nathan was a freshman; we were looking for awesome young boys to be involved in our training program. It can often be difficult to find gentlemen that age who are ready for this type of challenge. It can also be difficult to find gentlemen that willingly want to participate. Nathan was overwhelmingly nominated by his peers to attend the retreat. After the training, he did an amazing job in the peer helping role and continued to have an impact on his peers."

Another teacher who had regular interaction with Nathan in the classroom and in athletics at Spring Hill High School, was Brent Smitheran, a long-time math teacher and basketball coach at Spring Hill. Once Nathan entered high school, Brent worked with Nathan as his mathematics teacher and also coached him in basketball.

"The thing I always stressed with Nathan," recalls Brent, "and all of the student athletes that I work with, is that you can only do your best, and accept the results of your best efforts, whatever they may be. If you go out and give your best effort, then no matter what the final outcome of a game, you can hold your head high."

Brent remembers Nathan as a driven student, who strove to be perfect in the classroom and on the basketball court. Sometimes, Brent said Nathan was so conscientious that he put too much pressure on himself in his efforts to be his best. Brent says that Nathan was always looking for ways to make a difference in the lives of his classmates and teammates while striving to be the best student athlete he could be on and off the court.

"What I remember most about Nathan is his kind heart. Nathan wanted everyone to feel valued, and he went out of his way to make sure he did that."

Brent spoke about having Nathan as a math student and Nathan's outstanding work ethic. "As I recall, Nathan finished out the math course he took with me with an incredibly high-grade percentage, something like a 98% average. He aced every test he took for me; yet, he would be in to see me before classes started almost every single morning to get help on the previous day's assignment. Nathan was not content to just get a good grade; he needed to fully understand everything about the content we were covering. If he had even the slightest hint of confusion, he made sure he fixed that.

"I think he feared those bits of confusion coming back to bite him at a later date, but I also felt like Nathan was just motivated by curiosity. He always seemed really fascinated by new concepts and making connections between them and the other things that we covered in class.

"He was such a fun kid to teach because he was always so eager to learn. Not only that, he was eager to help others learn as well. I can remember him often spending his time in class helping one of his friends rather than doing his own work. There is one time in particular that I remember, when we had an away basketball game that night. Nathan did not work on his own assignment during class one bit. Nathan spent every minute of class that day working with this one student because I was busy helping a few others. He had to do his entire assignment after we got home from the away game, most likely at 10:30 at night. And then the next morning he came in early to ask me his daily questions. Nathan was the kind of student who makes you want to be a teacher. That kind of passion for learning and drive makes you want to be a better teacher because those type of students deserve it."

Brent also recalled another occasion when Nathan went out of his way to help a student at Spring Hill. Nathan was on his way home one day, when he noticed a family new to the area with a boy his age, moving furniture into their home in Spring Hill. Nathan stopped and introduced himself to this family, to see if they needed any help. According to Brent, Nathan spent the rest of the day helping them bring in boxes and furniture. Brent recalls how this new kid and his family were blown away that a boy whom they had never met, would go out of his way to help complete strangers. During that day, the new kid and Nathan formed a friendship.

Brent says that this young man Nathan befriended became a student at Spring Hill, and that this new student had a fairly abrasive personality that, at times, alienated him from the other students. The student was new to the area and as is the case with many high school age kids who have to relocate to a new school the transition for this young man was difficult. Brent says he would often become frustrated, and he tended to lash out at other people, even though they were not the cause of his troubles.

By the end of his time in high school, many of this new student's peers had pretty much had enough of him and just avoided him as much as they could, except for Nathan. Brent says, "Nathan would just take this student's negative comments with a smile and laugh them off. There were times when this student would make comments that created tension in class and the room would go silent.

"You could cut the tension with a knife, but before anyone else could respond Nathan would pop in some comment to turn what was said into a joke and completely diffuse the situation. He'd usually move over near this student and there would be a private conversation and some peer tutoring that would go on, and by the end of the period all would be well."

Brad Reinking is another veteran teacher at Spring Hill High School. He also worked with Nathan as a basketball coach. During the four years Nathan played for Brad, Brad came to know Nathan as a student and as a teammate to coaches and players in the locker room. Brad said he was impressed with the way Nathan carried himself off the basketball court as well.

"Nathan had such a silent, positive impact on everyone. His continuous smile and positive gait as he walked the halls was unique. Nathan presented a confidence without arrogance that was rare and idolized by others.

"During part of the time that I coached Nathan I also had my son as a player on the basketball team with Nathan. Nathan was a junior when my son was a freshman. My son had the utmost respect for Nathan. Not because they were buddies, but because of how Nathan treated my son. My son always felt comfortable that Nathan was going to treat him well even as an underclassman.

"I will never forget all the games of horse he and I played after practice together. Nathan was always one of the last ones to leave the floor when practice was over.

"Nathan was outgoing, assertive and positive. He was not judgmental by any means. Nathan did not think of or treat any kids differently. He was approachable to all who knew him. He was genuine. Nathan was not one to ever get caught up in other people's drama."

Nic Madelen was a young teacher/coach who was just beginning his teaching career at Spring Hill when he coached Nathan as a member of the varsity football team.

"Nathan was a special one-of-a-kind kid, mature well beyond his years. I coached him for three seasons, his sophomore, junior and senior years. Nathan was popular, well-liked and attractive. Nathan was a really good athlete. He played multiple sports, football and basketball.

"One of the things I remember most about Nathan, was that he just treated people well. He was not a 'rah, rah,' kind of a guy. He was a good athlete but he did not flaunt his abilities. Nathan was a very humble and kind person.

"He was a lead-by-example kind of kid. He was a quiet leader; I would describe Nathan as more of an introvert. He was very supportive of his teammates. Nathan demonstrated servant leadership in the locker room and at school.

"He was a good-looking athletic kid, very good student, but you did not see him hold himself up above others the way you sometimes see kids that age do in high school. Nathan was mature enough to not be caught up in the peer pressure of trying to standout or be recognized. He was humble and kind to everyone.

"And when you talked to Ron and to Nathan, the way they talked they were so much alike, the way they treated people. They were both so selfless, always thinking about helping other people. You could see that Nathan was the spitting image of his father."

8

Kevin Han and Ron Stiles grew up together in Spring Hill, Kansas. When they met, Kevin's father was the principal at Spring Hill High School. The boys were best friends and childhood classmates who went to grade school together from their second through their sixth-grade school years. They were in the same Cub Scout Troop. They played little league baseball together, and spent the night at each other's homes.

Ron remembers that Kevin's family had a shuffle board in the basement of their house where the boys would play in the winter whenever the weather was too cold for them to play outside. When Kevin was eleven years old, he and his family moved away from Spring Hill, and the two boys lost track of each other.

"I first met Ron when my family moved to Spring Hill when I was in the second grade, and we went from second grade to sixth grade together until my family moved to southeast Kansas. I would consider Ron my best friend while we lived in Spring Hill. We were childhood friends, we played ball together, did Cub Scouts and all the things you do when you are kids."

Then one day in the spring of 2008, 43 years later, after traveling from their home in Topeka, Kansas to Kansas City, Kevin and his wife, Rhonda, decided to drive over to Spring Hill and look Ron up. Once they reached Spring Hill, Kevin and Rhonda drove over to the Stiles' home on the family farm where Ron grew up, the same home where Ron's parents, Robert and Catherine Stiles, still lived. A few minutes after

Kevin and Rhonda arrived, Catherine Stiles called over to Ron's house. When Ron answered the phone Catherine said, "Guess who just showed up at our door?"

"Once our family left Spring Hill in 1966," Kevin said, "I didn't see Ron again for a long, long time. I moved to Topeka after I graduated from college and then one day we were in Kansas City and we had finished doing whatever we were doing and we had nothing else going on so I said to Rhonda, 'why don't we see if we can look Ron up?' It had been over 40 years since I had last seen him. I knew where his parents lived, and I knew from talking to my parents that they were still there. We drove over there and stopped by his parents' house and asked if Ron was around. Well, he happened to live only a mile or so away. So, he came over to his parent's house and we chit-chatted a little bit. It was good to see him again."

This was the first time Ron and Kevin had spoken since grade school. There was a lot of catching up to do and the friends visited for a while spending some long overdue time together. Once their visit ended, they exchanged contact information and parted ways once again.

A few months later, one night during basketball season that next school year, Ron was going to be in Topeka, attending a basketball game where Nathan and the Spring Hill team would be playing a local Topeka high school. Ron reached out to see if Kevin could meet him at the basketball game. But Kevin could not go to the game that night because he was already scheduled to volunteer with Kairos Torch, a Christian mentoring program, at the Kansas Juvenile Correctional Complex.

"We wanted to go and meet Ron at the basketball game and watch Nathan play but we were not able to make it because as it turns out we were busy that night with the Kairos Torch Prison Ministry. I didn't tell him that we were involved in the prison ministry at the time because I didn't think it was pertinent."

For the previous four years Kevin and Rhonda had volunteered with the Kairos Torch Youth Ministry at the Kansas Juvenile Correction Complex near their home in Topeka, Kansas.

"The juvenile center where we minister is the only maximum-security juvenile facility in the state. They are not messing around there. It is steel and concrete, and when the doors slam behind you, it is noisy, it is definitely a prison. The boys volunteer to be a part of Kairos. They also have to be selected or approved by the officers and the administration or the chaplain, so there is an approval process for them to participate. The young men range in age from 13 to 21 ½ and we have had the whole gamut of ages participating."

Ron Stiles and Kevin Han

9

Mike Reynolds and Nathan met while they were in high school. Nathan and Natalie went to high school in Spring Hill; Mike went to high school 10 miles away in Paola, Kansas. They became friends when Nathan and Natalie started attending the youth group at Lighthouse Presbyterian Church in Paola.

Hillsdale was a small church with only a few teenagers attending at that time, and Hillsdale's pastor, Laurie Johnston's husband, Kirk Johnston, was the pastor at Lighthouse Church. To help create a strong youth program that would reach teens in both communities, Laurie encouraged the kids from Hillsdale to meet with the teenagers in the youth program at Lighthouse. The churches combined their two youth groups together into the Lighthouse Youth Group.

Not long after the two churches merged their youth group programs together, the youth pastor at Lighthouse resigned to take a position with another Christian organization in the area. When that happened, there was a period of transition when Lighthouse Church did not have a youth pastor. It was during that transitional period when Mike and the Johnston's oldest son, Luke, along with Nathan, approached Pastor Kirk about the three of them assuming more of a leadership role within the youth group. During that time with Pastor Kirk and Pastor Laurie's guidance, the three boys and some of the other kids in the program began to lead the group in a weekly Bible study and other activities. Mike says that they would sometimes have up to 50 or 60 kids at their youth group meetings.

There was an open field next door to the Johnston's house where they would host the kids over at their home a night or two a week. It was there in that vacant lot where the kids would play Frisbee and other outdoor games. Afterwards the kids would form a circle in the backyard around their back deck, and talk about the Bible, and study scripture together.

"Teenage years are the most formative years of our lives," Mike said as he reflected on the time the kids spent together in youth group. "The world today is in such a cluster now. Those Wednesday night youth group meetings were a consistent, safe place where we could meet and support each other. That is very important for teens who are trying to find their way in the world; relationships at that age are everything.

"There was a core group of teenagers in that youth group who were growing in their faith, and we were not ashamed to tell people about Jesus. We did the best we could as teenagers to share the message of Jesus, and it worked. We had kids in that youth group who didn't necessarily come from families who were at the time attending church, and yet they came and were a part of our youth group and went with us to church. As teenagers sometimes we may think we can't make that big of a difference, but you can. And if parents want their kids to be a Christian, the parents need to be involved in church too, they need to model it.

"To build strong relationships there has to be communication. In order for a relationship to flourish, you don't need screen time; you need face to face time. In that youth group we formed a camaraderie that would not have happened any other way."

Mike described the experience of being a part of the youth group at Lighthouse as life-changing. "We have a whole lot better time in this life if we do life together. Life can be very hard sometimes, and life is always better when we don't try to live life alone.

"I would use the analogy of a campfire to illustrate the importance of relationships and community. When you pull a stick that is burning out of a campfire, that single stick will burn for a while on its own. But, if that stick remains away from the fire for long, the fire in that stick will burn out. That is what happens when we try to live life on our own. If we do that for long, our fire and passion will burn out. That is why community in youth groups and in churches is so important."

Over the years Mike, Luke and Nathan developed very close friendships. Mike says the three boys hung out together away from church too, doing things teenage boys do.

"We would drive over to Nathan's house and I would be hanging out the passenger window of Luke's car with some loud music playing, typical teenage stuff. We would go off and do what I would call 'escapades' together. Just spending time together. We would go play basketball, hang out at the pool, go out to an open field and hit golf balls off into the distance to see who could hit the ball the farthest, just being teenagers together, living life together. I remember times when we would shoot off Roman candles in Nathan's backyard, workout in the basement, watch movies, and we would make these stupid YouTube videos, fun stuff teenage boys will do. We spent a lot of time together just hanging out."

The boys also shared a love of music. Later they would form a Christian rock band, Awakening. Once the boys formed the band, they began to practice making music and even writing songs together.

"The Stiles family was an extended family for me in many ways. I spent a lot of time at their house, over the years Nathan and I did a lot together. The thing I remember most about Nathan was his distinctly committed character; who he was as a person. Nathan took his relationship with God very seriously. He was confident in who he was. Nathan and I would support each other to read the Bible and then we would discuss what we read together. We all need people in our lives that will hold us accountable, Nathan was that person for me. We all need relationships like that in our lives."

Nathan and Mike Reynolds

10

It was a snowy winter day in Kansas as Josie Stiles drove to an introductory meeting for people who were considering participation in an overseas mission trip to Africa, hosted by a local mission's program, Uganda N.O.W. As Josie drove to the meeting, she was considering the possibility of accompanying Uganda Now on the organization's upcoming mission trip in the summer of 2010. On the drive over that day Josie was not sure if she would commit to being a part of the trip, but she felt a call to missions and a desire within her to do something to help the people of Uganda.

Josie is an attractive, articulate and gifted young woman, with a heart for sharing the Gospel message. In her role as a high school teacher at Olathe East High School, Josie has the opportunity to invest her gifts into teaching young people.

When Josie arrived at the meeting that wintry day, she found that she was the first person other than the meeting's hosts to arrive. Once Josie came into the building and introduced herself, the local spokesperson who was hosting the meeting was thrilled she had come, because Josie says in their words, "we need teachers."

After the meeting Josie prayerfully considered attending the trip to Uganda. Later that year in the summer of 2010, she decided to volunteer for the trip to Uganda, and says the experience has had a profound impact on her life.

Later after returning from the trip to Uganda, Josie wrote a thank you letter to the people who had gifted her in support of her trip. She beautifully expressed her thanks to her supporters, and shared some of her memories from her experience.

"Your support of me shows every Ugandan that Americans care about them and that God has not left them or forsaken them. They repeatedly said "thank you," to me over the weeks I was there, tears of gratitude often accompanied their words of appreciation. Seeing adults full of joy like a child on Christmas morning was a common sight in Uganda.

"Every person that helped me needs to know the true appreciation from the Ugandans. They wanted to make certain I tell you what a difference the help of the Americans has made to them. I'm starting to tear up as I remember how thankful they were to us. They cried, hugged, dropped to their knees, and repeatedly said thank you. I appreciate your support more than I can express, and they appreciate it more than I can express for them."

While in Uganda Josie and the other trip participants worked closely with their Ugandan born host, Deo Musisi. Deo grew up on the island and was blessed with the ability to learn quickly, resulting in academic scholarships which allowed Deo to attend secondary school and later the university level. Now Deo speaks many languages and is an international businessman. Deo loves the Lord and wants to help the people where he grew up to have a means to better support themselves by teaching them trades and life skills while sharing the Gospel message.

Deo has a heart for vulnerable children. In 1992, Deo started what he would describe as, "a small ram-shacked place," to teach children English, which later turned into a worship and praise center on Busagazi Island. Then in 2007, Deo met a young American, Laura Holler, and this meeting later gave birth to Uganda Now.

While in Uganda Josie worked as one of the leaders in teacher workshops on Busagazi Island. Meanwhile, others on the Uganda Now team held Vacation Bible school with students. Once the instructional part of their day ended, the team worked together to provide meals for the students and the Ugandan teachers.

"I can't explain the feeling of dishing out beans and rice to face after face," Josie continues, "realizing this one meal a day is a treat they don't always have. This memory has stayed with me more than any other from the trip."

It was later in the summer of 2010, after returning from her trip to Uganda, Josie was at a family birthday celebration where she discussed with Nathan some of her memories and experiences from her trip to Uganda. As Nathan and Josie discussed her mission trip that day, they talked about some of the people Josie met and the needs of the Ugandans. As their conversation continued, Josie shared with Nathan the importance of finding a way of getting more Bibles shipped to the people of Uganda, so that more of them could read God's Word and help the mission team there to reach more people for Christ.

11

According to everyone who knew them, Nathan and his younger sister, Natalie, were very close. Natalie says that like most kids their age, their relationship had the typical brother-sister complications of fighting, tattling and teasing each other. However, in other ways, Natalie and Nathan's relationship was very different.

"Nathan was one of my best friends, and I mean seriously best friend. Our relationship had become a let's go on a double date, match on nerd day for spirit week, say 'Hi,' and hug in the hallway at school everyday type of friendship. More importantly we could talk about anything with each other.

"Nathan was a person who was very comfortable in his own skin," Natalie recalls. "Even though he was an athlete and a popular kid, he could at times be nerdy too. He had a multifaceted personality, he would do things that for most people would seem strange at times, but he was so well thought of by his peers that it was natural for him to do things that might seem nerdy to other people, and still be accepted."

Natalie is a tall, athletic, attractive young lady, who is very bright and has an engaging personality like the rest of her family.

Katie George, a guidance counselor at Spring Hill High School, described Natalie as, "an incredible young lady. Natalie and I still stay in touch today. She is sweet, charismatic, genuine and tenderhearted. She always has been true to herself and displayed strong moral values."

Loree Hieber, who was Natalie and Nathan's Sunday school teacher, remembers that Natalie and Nathan were according to her, "collecting grandparents" at Hillsdale Church.

"Most Sunday mornings Natalie and Nathan would come in the kitchen and give hugs to all the older ladies in the church, and the ladies loved it. They were very special young people," says Loree.

Courtney Swope, a close friend of Nathan's, described Natalie this way, "Nathan thought the world of Natalie. Nathan believed that Natalie would accomplish great things in her life. Natalie is an incredible girl; who knows exactly who she is. She is such a fun person to be around."

Natalie says that one of the most important conversations she and Nathan ever had happened the day after they attended a movie one evening that was shown in a local church, "To Save a Life."

The following day as Nathan and Natalie were driving to school together the two of them talked about the movie and how they wanted their lives to be different, that they wanted to make a difference for Christ in the world. They agreed that they did not want their passion for God to fade away. As the two of them drove along they committed to each other to live for God in a life-changing way. They were determined to get their classmates in on it also, to live for God and help make a change in their school, church and community for Christ.

12

Grace Community Church is located in Spring Hill, Kansas. Many of the kids from Spring Hill High School attended church at Grace. At Grace Community Church, Senior Pastor Joel Atwell realized that oftentimes Christian children may find it difficult to live out their faith in a secular world. That Christian teens may not always fit in with the social culture of their classmates, and at times they may be excluded from some activities by their peers because of their faith.

Joel made an effort to support the kids in their church by encouraging them to build relationships with other Christian kids and teens their age. Joel remembers that Nathan was very interested in learning more about the Bible. "He was also interested in learning new ways he could live out his faith. Nathan and I often spoke about Nathan's concerns regarding the faith life of his friends, and how we might be able to reach kids for Christ in Nathan's school, and the community at large."

Doug Atteberry was working as a youth minister on the staff of Grace Community Church in the summer of 2010 when Natalie and Nathan began attending the youth group meetings at Grace. Going to the Grace youth group meetings gave Nathan and Natalie an opportunity to spend time with their Spring Hill High School classmates while still keeping their relationships with the youth at the Hillsdale and Lighthouse Churches.

"You could see right away that Nathan and Natalie were very close." Doug continues, "I remember that there was a 'twin day' at Spring Hill High School and they both dressed up as nerds for school that day. You don't see many siblings that are close enough to do something like that."

Doug said he would often play basketball with the kids who attended the Grace youth group meetings. Doug had a son who was a few years younger than Nathan, and they and the other kids would play pick-up basketball games together. Playing in those pick-up basketball games was where Doug came to know Nathan on a more personal level.

As Doug remembers, "Nathan was very polite, always conscious of other people's feelings. I remember times when Nathan would apologize for fouling me in a pick-up basketball game."

Doug described Nathan as one of those kids who would naturally gravitate to younger kids and mentor them. "It was not unusual for Nathan to reach out and invest himself in the younger kids.

"Nathan was the kind of young man you would want your son to be like and you would want your daughter to marry. The reason Nathan was the person he became was a result of his relationship with God and the time he spent in God's Word.

"Nathan's life was proof of the transforming power of the Gospel. The Bible teaches us about the different paths available to us, the path that leads to death and the path that leads to life. Nathan chose the path that leads to life. As Nathan pursued Christ, life was flowing out of Nathan and into the lives of others."

13

The Awakening band that Nathan, Mike and Luke started was continuing to practice together in the spring of 2010. By this time the boys were beginning to write some of their own music. Nathan had a beautiful singing voice and loved to sing. He had been involved with church choir for several years by now as well as being involved in the Madrigals choral program at school. Nathan and Luke Johnston had already co-written an original song for the band, titled "Break-In."

With all the exciting things that were happening in the band, Nathan was leaning toward not playing football his senior year. Nathan had told Ron that he was considering not playing football in the fall, and focusing on being a part of the band and working part time with Ron at the oil company in the afternoons after school, and then playing varsity basketball in the winter.

It was later near the end of that summer, a few weeks before football practice was to begin, that the Spring Hill varsity football coaches organized a father-son softball game. The game was meant to be a bonding time for the players, dads and coaches. Ron says that there were not enough dads signed up to fill out a team, so some of the boys volunteered to play on the dad's team, and Nathan was one of them.

It was shortly after this softball game that Nathan learned that he had been elected as a team captain of the football team. Even though Nathan told Ron he was not crazy about the idea of playing football his senior season, Nathan decided to go ahead and play anyway. Nathan decided to play football because he felt a commitment to his teammates. He had grown up playing football with this same group of boys for years, and he did not want to let his team down.

"Nathan loved his buddies," Ron recalled. "I told him that if he decided to skip the football season and sing with the band instead of playing football he could just work at my business. His buddies wanted him on the football team with them and Nathan loved his friends. He was not wild about it, but he said he was going to play anyway. It was at that point too when Nathan had to choose to leave the band because if he had kept singing with the group it would not have allowed him the time to be on the football team.

"When we played the softball game that day Nathan had quite a game hitting and he fielded the ball quite well too. I used to have some fair speed myself when I was a kid, and I used all I had that day. I left the field that evening having pulled two muscles. I had trouble getting around for a week after that game. Not sure what the score was, but we won!

"There was a picture taken by one of the moms who had a son playing in the game that day. Nathan and I are standing side by side together in that photograph. That picture meant a lot to me then, but I had no idea how much it would really mean until later. The picture of Nathan and me that was taken that day is priceless to me. Little did I know at that time that our new father-son team was about to begin; we would go from a father and son playing on a softball field together trying to win a game, to what would later turn into a father-son team working for Jesus."

14

In the fall of 2010, Travis Bosse was a rising junior at Spring Hill High School. That summer before school started, Travis was looking for a girlfriend. But not just any girl; that fall before classes started Travis began to pray that God would bring a girl into his life that he could have a special relationship with. Not just a fling, the kind of relationships you typically see in high schools. Travis wanted to meet a girl that he could have a relationship with that was intentional, the kind of girl that he could potentially marry one day.

After Travis began to pray for God's guidance he was led to Nicole VanDaele. Travis remembers that once school started, he and Nicole had four of their seven classes together. Before that school year Travis and Nicole had never been in a single class together. It was then that Travis approached Nicole, and the two began talking. Over time their relationship developed.

Travis remembers as a kid growing up in grade school that he and his family did not go to church much, maybe once or twice a year on special occasions or holidays; but that all began to change when Travis was in the second grade.

"During my second-grade year my father developed a rare form of cancer. During those years he took chemotherapy treatments and afterwards things would appear to be improving, but after the treatments he would relapse and the cancer would return. During that time my dad had to face death, and when that happened, he began to take his faith more seriously. That is when my dad committed his life to Christ and chose to follow him, and that changed our family pretty drastically."

Travis remembers that up until that time his dad had a really bad temper and then all of a sudden once he accepted Christ he didn't.

"From that point on we began to go to church regularly, but at that time I was still not that interested in church. I went with my parents but it wasn't until later in high school participating in youth group that I became more interested in God. During his middle school years Travis and his family started going to a different church where he says, "They had a really good youth pastor. That is when we began to have some people other than our parents begin to invest themselves in us. They were loving us well in our youth group, and they taught us about the Bible and cared well for us."

Then during the summer between his freshman and sophomore year of high school Travis went on a mission trip to work at a summer camp for special needs people, kids and adults. It was there that Travis saw something he had not seen before.

"I saw these people working in this camp loving these special needs people very well. These volunteers who were working in the camp, they had smiles on their faces, and they were very intentional serving these people. I remember thinking 'that was really cool,' and I thought I would like to be like these Christian volunteers."

Another thing Travis witnessed during his mission trip for the first time was that every morning at this camp they would have set devotional time for the volunteers and the participants. Travis remembers that he would see these people going off by themselves and take their Bibles with them. Travis says that he would go too, even though at that time he did not know what he was supposed to do.

Later during the trip one night, Travis felt inspired to get his Bible out and read it. Travis took out a flashlight, and underneath the cover of his small cot type bunk bed, he read his Bible. Travis says that was the first time he chose to read the Bible on his own. "I do not know if that was the point where I felt I was saved, but that was the first time that I began to see God working in my life personally."

Nicole went to church some too when she was growing up, but she says she basically went because her mom wanted her to. "I really didn't care that much about church at that time. I actually went to youth group down at Hillsdale with Natalie and Nathan for a very short time. I didn't think at that time that God was relevant, I questioned if God existed. I didn't think making a decision about God was that urgent."

Nicole remembers thinking making a decision about God was something she could deal with later. She says during that time she was dealing with some anger issues as well and she was not very trusting of people. "I put a lot of my identity in school, how I did there, because I did well in school. My identity was so caught up in how I performed in school at that time that if I did not do well on a test or if I would lose a homework assignment, I would have a slight panic attack."

Nicole says when Travis first began showing interest in her during their junior year of high school, she was not that interested in a relationship. But once Travis began to pursue her, she could see that there was something different about this boy.

"Right off the bat I could tell Travis was different than the other guys who had been interested in me before. Just the way he treated me. I remember one time when I cussed in front of him and he looked at me and said, 'You don't need to do that.' And Travis was very modest, which is odd for a 16-year-old guy to be modest. Travis was definitely different. He talked to me a lot about church, and me going to church with him. At that point I was like, 'drop it.' Church is really not that big of a deal. I go, randomly. At that time, I was really not that interested in church."

The weeks passed and the school year progressed, and as they did, Travis continued to pursue Nicole.

"Travis asked me to go with him to Homecoming, so we went to Homecoming together. About a week after the Homecoming Dance, I sent Travis a text and asked him, 'Are we officially dating?'"

Travis responded, "Yes."

15

In the late summer of 2010 football drills began in Spring Hill. Football practices always begin with a few days of conditioning drills as are mandatory for high school football teams. During these conditioning days there is no contact, blocking or tackling drills. The players dress out in shorts, t-shirts and helmets as they run through agility and conditioning drills in the hot August sun.

After a couple of weeks of conditioning practices, teams are allowed to begin dressing out in full gear. It is during these first weeks of practice in pads that teams begin to install their offensive and defensive playbooks. This is the part of the high school football season when team scrimmages begin and players compete for starting roles and playing time in the upcoming season.

It did not take long before Nathan had his first serious injury of his senior season of football. Nathan broke his hand the first day of contact drills and had to have a plate surgically placed in his hand. Due to this injury he was not able to play the first several weeks of the season. During those weeks Nathan continued to faithfully attend practice. Nathan would most days dress out in full gear and run wind sprints on the sidelines while his teammates practiced. He lifted weights and supported his team as best he could, doing whatever he was able to do to encourage the efforts of his teammates on the field.

Some of Nathan's coaches would later remark that they were inspired by Nathan's commitment to practice even though he was injured. As a team captain and senior one can understand how a committed young man like Nathan would want to set a good example of leadership for his teammates. After all, that is what we are taught as young men to do, to be someone others can count on when the chips are down, and to always set a good example. Leading by example was a character trait that Nathan felt was important, not just on the football field or in the locker room, but in all aspects of his life. When he injured his hand, he did what came naturally, he came to practice every day and led by example. He practiced within the limitations of his injury, and set a good example for the other players, so that he would be ready when the time came for him to go back on the field again and help his team.

It would be September 24th before Nathan was able to return to the field. He played that first game back with a wrapped arm. Spring Hill lost the game but Nathan held his own, still, it was frustrating for Ron to watch Nathan play with an injured hand. The morning after the game as Nathan was sitting at the kitchen counter eating his breakfast, Ron and Nathan talked about how things were going with the football team. Then, as Ron and Nathan were alone there in the kitchen, Ron had this strange feeling that he needed to talk with Nathan about him quitting the football team.

"As I was standing by the refrigerator talking to him," Ron said, "I felt something that said to me, *'Tell Nathan it's okay to quit!'* Strange! I felt it stronger once again. *'Tell Nathan it's okay to quit!'* Well I gave in and told Nathan, 'I know you are not a quitter, but it is okay to quit. Your hand is not healed, and besides, basketball will be starting before you know it and you love playing basketball.' He said nothing and needless to say, he did not quit. As Nathan left the room, whoever or whatever that thought was, I said to myself, *'What was that all about? It's not like playing football will kill him.'*

"Later on, I would understand how important telling him it was okay to quit was going to be."

16

Courtney Swope is a lovely, athletic young lady with an engaging personality, who played volleyball and basketball at Spring Hill High School. After graduating from Spring Hill High School, Courtney attended Neosho County Community College for one year where she was a member of the women's basketball team. She then transferred to York College in Nebraska, where she played the role of shooting guard on the women's varsity basketball team for three years. Two of Courtney's cousins were also members of York College Women's Basketball team.

Courtney and Nathan had known each other since they were in the sixth grade together. But in the fall of 2010 their relationship began to change. They were becoming boyfriend and girlfriend.

Over the next several months Nathan and Courtney's relationship continued to grow. Then on a Friday night, October 1st, during halftime of the Spring Hill Homecoming football game, Nathan and Courtney stood side by side as members of the Homecoming court. Nathan as a King nominee, and Courtney, a Homecoming Queen candidate.

During the halftime ceremony, as the two of them were standing there on the field together anxiously awaiting the results to be announced, Courtney says, "Nathan was making a list of all the other guys who he thought would be recognized instead of him. That was the way he was. He always saw the good in everyone else."

As is the tradition in many homecoming ceremonies, the parents of the young people nominated as king and queen candidates escorted their children onto the field.

"The Homecoming game came on October 1st, and Nathan was a king candidate. Not only was Nathan a king candidate, but the girl he was falling head over heels for was a queen candidate." Ron continues, "It made for a wonderful moment as Connie and I walked him on the field, as Nathan was crowned Homecoming King, and his new found girlfriend Courtney, was chosen Homecoming Queen. What an evening.

"Little did I know that a year later, I would be handing the crown for Nathan to the new Homecoming King, and Nathan's sister Natalie, would be crowned the new Homecoming Queen. Nathan was always very proud of his sister and he would have been again."

Later that night after the game ended, Nathan and Courtney went out to eat and celebrate with their friends from school. Courtney remembers, "After we were crowned at the Homecoming game, we went to the IHOP to eat, and I was telling Nathan he should wear his crown, but Nathan was so humble he did not want to bring attention to himself. That is who he was.

"Nathan was a really great guy, humble, sincere and supportive. He was the stud athlete at school but he was never boastful about himself. He was mature beyond his years. Nathan was a person who saw the good in everyone. Nathan was intelligent, handsome, had a beautiful singing voice, and at the same time he could be a real goofball too. Nathan had a very diverse personality. Whenever you were with Nathan, he made you feel like he was focused only on you."

During the week after the Homecoming game, Nathan complained of a headache one day at practice, so the coaches immediately took him out of practice and referred him to be examined by a physician. Connie took him to the doctor where it was determined that Nathan did indeed have a concussion. The scan came up negative, but as a per concussion protocol,

Nathan would be held out of practice and games for the next several weeks.

Nathan and Courtney as Homecoming King and Queen

17

For the next three weeks Nathan, as a precautionary measure, did not participate in any football practices or games. Only after having additional tests run and his headaches subsided, was Nathan allowed by the doctors to return to the field again to play. The next game Nathan participated in was October 22nd. This would be the last home game of the season for Spring Hill, and Senior Night for the players and their parents.

Connie had left home early that evening to go by the store to get Nathan a new calculator as she and Ron thought Nathan had lost his. Later on, Ron and Connie would learn that what had really happened to Nathan's calculator was that someone in Nathan's class had needed one, and Nathan gave him his. Since Connie was going by the store to pick up a calculator, Ron told Connie that he would stop by his father's house and pick up his dad on the way to the stadium and meet her at the game. Being Senior Night, Ron was looking forward to walking Nathan once more across the field. Thinking the Senior Night ceremony would be during halftime Ron did not arrive to the game early.

"As I got out of my truck in the parking lot, I heard Nathan's name being announced. The ceremony started before the game and I had missed it. Walking into the stadium someone I knew said to me, *you missed it.*' I had such a strange, mad, upset feeling come over me. As I watched the start of the game, I began to boil. I missed it! Poor me! Whose fault was it? Someone should have told me! It was strange, so strange

61

that I would be so mad that I started to think maybe God was trying to tell me something, but what? So, I began to reason we would have basketball senior parent night and I would be there on time."

It was a light kind of rain in the air that night, and as Ron sat there in the misty cool night air, he continued to fume over missing the opening ceremony for Nathan. Ron says it took him until the third quarter to get calmed down from missing the ceremony and not being able to walk on the field that night with Nathan.

"I felt like standing up and yelling at everyone," Ron remembered. "It still gnawed at me as I continued to reason, 'What is God trying to tell me?'

"Later that night once the game ended, Nathan said he was feeling good and he was glad to be playing again."

18

The final game of the 2010 football season was played on Thursday night, October 28th in Osawatomie, Kansas against Osawatomie High School. The game was being played on a Thursday night instead of Friday because the Kansas State High School football playoffs were to begin the next week.

Osawatomie, Kansas is only a short 20-minute drive down Highway 169 from Spring Hill. With the close proximity of the two schools many of the players, coaches and fans from each community knew each other and, in some cases, very well.

This would be the final game of the season for both teams since neither team had qualified for the playoffs, so this would be the last time the senior football players from each school would play in a high school football game. As anyone who has ever participated in team sports will tell you, it is an emotional experience when you are a senior, and you take off your school's jersey for the last time. With all the emotion of the season coming to a close, the players on both teams were determined to give it their all so they could end their season on a winning note.

As the football season had progressed the Osawatomie team developed a potent offensive passing attack that featured their star quarterback, Seth Jones. Seth was also a standout performer on defense for Osawatomie where he played strong safety. On the other sideline, Spring Hill featured a strong running attack on offense, passing the ball only sparingly and running the football nearly every play.

It was a cool crisp night, and many of the spectators, players and coaches would later remark that it was a perfect night for a high school football game. As the teams arrived at the stadium and prepared for the opening kickoff, there was an additional air of excitement in the stadium as it was also Senior Night for the Osawatomie players.

Dave French was an assistant coach on the sidelines for Osawatomie that night. Dave's coaching responsibility was primarily to work with the offensive and defensive linemen. Before the game Dave remembers standing outside the Osawatomie locker room and seeing some of the Spring Hill offensive players coming out of their team locker room for their pregame warm-up and walking past him on their way to the field.

"I remember that night seeing their running backs and thinking there were some good-looking athletes filling out those pads. I knew this was going to be a good game; it was a beautiful evening for football."

Later when Dave took the Osawatomie offensive linemen out onto the field for the pregame warm-up, he remembered seeing Nathan, number "44" running drills on the other side of the field for Spring Hill, noticing right away that he looked powerful and fast.

Dave's attention then turned back to his team getting his boys ready for their last game of the season. This was an emotional night for Dave personally, because a lot of these players that were seniors, playing in their final high school game, Dave had coached or known since they were little boys. In addition to Dave's relationship with this group of seniors, Dave's son, Andy French, was a member of this senior Osawatomie class. Andy had played sports with this group of seniors for years. But sadly, Andy's life and the lives of the French family had taken an unexpected turn in the past year.

Due to a medical condition, a little over six months earlier in the spring of 2010, Andy had a pace-maker implanted in his heart and as a result of this surgery Andy's football career was over.

Andy had been the Osawatomie starting middle linebacker the season before, but now since his surgery, Andy could no longer play football. This Senior Night, Andy would stand on the sidelines wearing his number "15" jersey proudly in support of his team.

Once the pregame warm-ups ended Dave did not go back into the locker room with the Osawatomie team before the game began as he normally would have. Instead Dave and his wife, Lori, came down on the sidelines where they walked with their son Andy, across the track in front of the hometown stadium crowd, as the seniors were recognized for their contributions to the Osawatomie football program.

"Andy was our third son to walk the walk before the final game of the season on Senior Night, and as was the case with our other boys, I felt much pride," said Dave.

The pregame proceedings progressed as they would on any other night. The two teams came back onto the field, and after the coin toss Spring Hill kicked off to Osawatomie to begin the game. After a short kickoff return, on the game's first offensive play from scrimmage, Seth Jones, who was playing quarterback for Osawatomie, dropped back to pass and threw a pass out toward the sideline that was tipped by a Spring Hill defender and into the Osawatomie's receiver's hands. Once the receiver caught the football, the Osawatomie player ran 59 yards for a touchdown. From that point on both teams scored on every possession of the first half. Seth remembers that neither team would punt the entire game.

Nic Madelen, who was an assistant coach for Spring Hill that night said, "It had been a long season for us; we were in a rebuilding year. Everything about the game that night was strange. From the beginning both teams moved the ball up and down the field the entire night. We ran the ball most every play and Osawatomie threw the ball nearly every play. Both teams would score at will."

Ron was sitting in the stands with Connie and Natalie. "As the game began it would not be long before you knew it would be a strange one," recalled Ron. "At the end of the first quarter the score was 24-22."

Ron remembers that as the game progressed and both teams continued to move the ball from one end of the field to the other, "I turned to a family that I knew who was sitting behind me and said, 'This has been such a strange football year that one of these days I am going to write a book about it.' After I said that I thought that was a strange thing to say, but, oh well, it kind of goes along with the year we have had. The game continued on that way as the score was rolling higher."

On the home team side of the field sitting high above the playing field in the coaches' press box, Chad Jones, an assistant coach for Osawatomie was calling the offensive plays. From his position above the field Chad remembers that the game was like a track meet, as both teams moved the ball with explosive offensive plays, one after another up and down the field in the first half.

"From the start of the game you could tell both teams were going to have trouble stopping each other." Chad continues, "Every time Spring Hill got the football it was a couple of long runs and then a touchdown. Nathan was running extremely hard and was doing amazing. He was running very tough and was very hard to tackle. Every time we got the football, we would run a pass play or two and score. Seth was playing amazing, as well. He was hitting almost every receiver in stride, and when no one was open he was running the football just as well. It was the most productive I think the two offenses had ever been."

"I was a sophomore that night," says Austin Chisam, who is now a teacher and coach for his alma mater, Osawatomie High School, as he reflected on the offensive fireworks during the first half of the game. "It was obviously very high scoring. I was playing receiver on offense and corner on defense. On defense, I remember we couldn't stop Nathan in that first half.

He ran all over us and we couldn't get a hold on him. It seemed as if every time Nathan ran for a touchdown, we would get the ball back and we would have a passing touchdown going back the other way. We were just trading scores for most of the first half. It was a hard-fought game as both teams were not going to end up making the playoffs, and we knew it would be our last game of the season on both sides. Nobody wants to lose the last game of the year and go out a loser. A football season is a long one, when you put in the weight room training, and all the summer workouts, and then the regular season practices. It takes a lot of grit, effort, and toughness to complete a whole season. That feeling was on the line of who is going to be the loser at the end of this thing. Our seniors were giving it everything they had, knowing it would be the last time they stepped on Lynn Dickey Field."

As the first half progressed, Nathan continued to run hard from his running back position. Nathan ran for 165 yards and scored two touchdowns on offense, as well as making several tackles while playing linebacker on defense. Then, somewhere around the three-minute mark before halftime, Nathan ran from the field to the Spring Hill sideline complaining of a severe headache, and within a matter of moments, Nathan collapsed on the sideline. With the fast-paced activity continuing on the field attracting the attention of the crowd, suddenly Nathan, who was shielded from view by the players and coaches, unaware to most everyone in the stadium, was now down on the sideline being attended to by the Spring Hill training staff.

"With about two minutes to go in the first half," Ron continued, "Natalie received a call that Nathan had collapsed on the sideline. Then she received another call to get there quick. From that point on it was like you were on a terrible ride that has no way of getting off."

As the game continued on the field, very few people in the stands could see that there was an injured player on the Spring Hill side of the field. Then, right before halftime, as

Dave was sitting in his position in the press box with Chad Jones, and the Osawatomie offense was driving the ball toward the south end of the field near the end zone, suddenly, out of the corner of his eye, Dave saw a coach from the Spring Hill side of the field come sprinting across the playing field to the Osawatomie sideline to get the team doctor. With the fast-paced game going on, and the fans looking in the other direction, the fans in the stands nor the players and referees officiating the game could see what had happened. The Spring Hill coach sprinting across the field reached the Osawatomie team doctor so quickly, that the game was not stopped and play on the field continued. It was then for the first time, from their position in the press box, that Dave and Chad could see what was happening. That is when they realized something was seriously wrong over on the Spring Hill sideline.

"That night, incredible football game, I was on the sidelines with the Osawatomie team, when right before halftime, Nathan becomes unconscious," Dr. Jeff Dorsett continues, "then I believe it was Ron or a member of the Spring Hill coaching staff that came over to our sideline and told us there was an injured player down on their sideline that needed attention. Soon after I reached the Spring Hill sideline Nathan was having a seizure. I had strong feelings for Nathan and his family as a doctor that night. Immediately we knew the seriousness of that situation. I had immensely deep feelings as a father that night too, for Nathan and his family. I had a son playing in the game for Osawatomie that night as well. We stabilized Nathan as we waited for paramedics to arrive."

As Nathan remained lying on the field moving just once as his mom Connie talked to him, Ron could see the look of concern from the doctor who was treating Nathan. Dr. Jeff Dorsett, the same doctor who had treated Ron with his ruptured appendix in that small clinic in Osawatomie all those years ago back in 1997.

With very few people realizing at this point that Nathan was down on the sideline and with only a minute or so to play in the half, Spring Hill had the ball again and was driving down field when Seth from his safety position made a big hit on a Spring Hill ball carrier very close to the Spring Hill sideline. Once the play was over, Seth and the Spring Hill player he tackled hopped up and went back across the field to their respective team's huddles.

After the play was over from Dave and Chad's point of view sitting in the press box, on the Osawatomie side of the field, they could see for the first time the player who was down on the Spring Hill sideline receiving medical attention from the trainers and Dr. Dorsett. Since the tackle happened right near where Nathan was down, they at first assumed that the player on the sideline had been injured by Seth's tackle. Everything just lined up perfectly to make it appear that was the case. Of course, later that night they found out that Nathan was already down and Seth had made the hit on a different Spring Hill player who just jumped right up and kept playing. But not having those details at that time it would be easy to see how someone sitting in the stands that night could have assumed Nathan's injuries might have come from that play.

The first half ended with Nathan still being treated on the field. Both teams left the field knowing there was an injured player on the Spring Hill sideline but none of them knew the extent of Nathan's injuries or the seriousness of the situation.

Once the teams exited the playing field, there were ambulances on the scene moving about quickly inside the stadium. As the situation with Nathan progressed the medical staff determined that it was necessary to call for a Life Flight helicopter to transport Nathan to Kansas University Medical Center. As the teams left the field and the players and coaches went into their respective locker rooms, the spectators in the stadium could see for the first time the seriousness of what was happening with Nathan just off the playing field.

Some of the Osawatomie players who were playing in the game that night remembered walking into the locker room at half time knowing that one of the Spring Hill running backs was hurt, but at that time they had no idea how serious Nathan's injuries were. They did not know that Nathan had suffered a head injury or the severity of it. As players and coaches in any contact sport realize, it's common place for players to have injuries, and that bumps and bruises are a part of athletics. But no one in either locker room realized the seriousness of what was happening on the sideline with Nathan and his family, or that what was occurring in the stadium that night would become a life changing event for everyone who was there.

Once what would have normally been the allotted time for the halftime to end came, the Osawatomie players and coaches left their locker room and began to enter the hallway leading back out onto the field. Dave French, who was at the front of the line standing alongside Seth Jones, was preparing to open the field house doors when they were met by the game officials. The referees told the Osawatomie coaches to hold their team in the locker room. Dave and Seth could see the look of concern on the officials' faces. The officials told Dave that a player from Spring Hill was being life-flighted from the field and the Osawatomie team needed to stay in the locker room until told to come out.

By this time the Osawatomie team had already spilled out into the hallway behind Dave and Seth, and they too could see everything that was happening on the other side of the field. Dave remembers there were emergency vehicles everywhere and red lights flickering all over the place. The entire team was in complete silence in the hallway as the young men from Osawatomie all stared out toward the field wondering what was going on. The team could now see all the ambulances on the field near the Spring Hill sidelines. Dave vividly recalls that the players and coaches were stunned by the presence of so many emergency responders. As the players and coaches stood shoulder-to-shoulder in silence in the hallway, the gravity of the situation began to sink in. Dave remembers, "No one from our vantage point could see exactly what was going on. We could not see the emotion of what was happening on the Spring Hill sideline, but we could feel it."

Moments later, Dave stepped out from the hallway to try and gather some additional information about the injured Spring Hill player. He then turned and looked behind him, back toward his Osawatomie team, where he saw the fear and concern in the eyes of his players. In a matter of minutes, the Life Flight helicopter took off from the field and hovered above.

"There were two communities there that night," Dave said, "with adults, mothers, fathers, kids; everyone was stunned. A beautiful, festive fall evening had suddenly turned into something that all parents dread when their children play sports - the possibility of serious injury."

As the helicopter flew above the stunned crowd, Dr. Dorsett made his way back to the Osawatomie locker room.

"I was very good friends with an Osawatomie assistant coach," Dr. Dorsett said, "and when the Osawatomie coach came out of the locker room after halftime, I told him that the situation was serious, and that we should pray for Nathan before beginning the second half. At a moment like that you realize that a football game is not that important. I remember this incredible sense of what a powerful God we have that evening, as I watched these young men on both teams and their coaches come together on the field kneeling and praying for Nathan."

Dave's wife, Lori, was sitting in the stands with a friend watching everything as it transpired on the field. "As time passed the situation became more serious. Then the helicopter came in and afterwards it was very quiet. After the halftime ended, the boys came out onto the field to pray for Nathan. Just as the boys were kneeling together on the field praying, this single bird flies in overhead from behind the bleachers where we were sitting. This bird then hovered above us, and flew back and forth above the stadium crowd. It then flew out over the field and hovered above the kneeling players as they prayed on the field for Nathan. It was all so quiet and surreal."

When Dave and Chad came back to the press box after halftime, sitting beside them in the Spring Hill press box, all the Spring Hill coaches were crying. They didn't have to say anything, Dave said, "We knew then how serious the situation was."

Once the players finished their prayer for Nathan there was a brief period of warmups before the game resumed. The play on the field was spirited in the second half as Spring Hill would go on to win the game. But for the players on the field and the people in the stands the rest of that night their minds were on Nathan and his family.

Earlier in the evening, Jim Hartsock and his son had attended a soccer game, where Jim's older son was playing in a Kansas State playoff game for the Spring Hill varsity soccer team. Once the game was over, Jim texted a friend who was at the football game to find out how the football game was going. "The Spring Hill football team was not having a very good season, but since Spring Hill was leading at halftime, we decided to drive the 20 minutes to watch the rest of the football game," says Jim. "When we arrived, all the emergency vehicles were on the football field and a helicopter was getting ready to land."

Seeing the ambulances and helicopter as they walked in, Jim's son said, "I hope nothing happened to Nathan."

Jim's son was in the 8th grade at the time, while Nathan was a senior, and Jim says his son really didn't know Nathan that well. While Jim thought it was an odd comment, the two of them kept walking to get into the stadium so they could find out what had happened. Upon arriving they quickly learned that Nathan was indeed the injured Spring Hill player.

Later that night as Jim and his son were driving home from the game, Jim asked his son, "When we were going into the stadium tonight why did you say you hoped nothing had happened to Nathan?"

His son replied, "Because any time I would see Nathan at a game or school activity, Nathan would always say 'hi' to me, and treat me like a regular kid, not a little 8th grader. Nathan was always nice to me."

"Waiting for the ambulance that night and then for Life Flight; everything just did not look good," Ron remembers. "As I stood there over Nathan, two feelings started to creep over me. 'Whose fault is it, and feeling sorry for myself if Nathan dies.' The same feelings I had less than a week before when I was late for Nathan's Senior Night. Was God with me, helping to calm me through my appendix ordeal? Was God telling me it was okay to leave the church? Was God having me tell Nathan it was okay to quit football? Was God getting me ready for the weak human feelings we can have? My trust in Jesus was headed for a whole new level that I really did not want and so confused about what to do.

"It all seemed like a strange ride with no way of getting off. Waiting on the ambulance and then Life Flight my mind was churning concerned about what was going to happen with Nathan. The one and only thing I knew for certain, is that Nathan would be in Heaven if he died this night. He had lived a life getting ready for this moment, but who knew it would come so soon. Life Flight arrived which seemed like a lifetime ago, and took off with our son to Kansas University Medical Center."

19

For the next hour Ron and the family drove to Kansas University Medical Center as Nathan was being transported by Life Flight. During the blur of a ride to the hospital the family all tried to remain upbeat, but Ron could feel everyone's concerns growing as they pressed on. Arriving at the hospital it did not take long before bad news started coming their way. As the hours passed, family and friends came into the hospital and were beside them as the news became more and more grim.

With two waiting rooms full and people standing along the hallways praying for Nathan, the news came from the doctors that Nathan would not survive. Ron recalls that KU Medical Center was wonderful to the family every step of the way, and this continued as the medical staff allowed time for group after group of Nathan's family members and friends to enter the hospital room and say goodbye to Nathan.

"The football game that had begun about 8 ½ hours earlier," Ron said, "was about to end as we stood beside our son and were told Nathan had died."

Once again, the waiting continued. Nathan had asked when he got his driver's license what being an organ donor meant and when Ron told him, Nathan agreed to be an organ donor. The stress on Nathan's body from his injuries caused his organs to suffer a lot of damage, but as Nathan would have wanted, the donation of his organs did happen so that he could help others, the final wishes of a selfless young man who had spent his life looking for ways to help other people.

"It was very hard to leave him, and walk out of the hospital that early Friday morning," Ron said, "but his grandpa Eldon was in another hospital recovering from a surgery he had, and we had to tell him before he saw it on the news. Nathan was grandpa Eldon's first grandchild and they had spent many wonderful days together, especially on the farm. It was hard news to deliver."

From there the family went home. Accompanied by their pastor Laurie Johnston, her pastor husband, Kirk, and their son and Nathan's friend, Luke, they made it back home. Ron said, "It was a very strange and lonely homecoming as we went through the house knowing Nathan would no longer be there."

As the family walked through their home that night Natalie remembered the feeling of emptiness that she experienced, "That feeling that could only be described as knowing something was missing. Is it possible to call a place home when it feels like that?"

Still trying to come to grips with all they had experienced in the last few hours; the family made their way downstairs to the basement where they saw Nathan's Bible on the end table and the imprint in the couch where he had been lying earlier that day reading the Bible. The day before, like every other day, Nathan had been in the Word.

Ron, Connie and Natalie knew that Nathan had taken the challenge from his Sunday school teacher, Loree Hieber, to read the Bible every day seriously. They understood that it was Nathan's commitment to read and study his Bible that shaped Nathan into the young man he was.

In the midst of the most difficult trial any parents and family could face, the loss of a child or sibling, the family leaned on their shared faith in God. Even though Nathan's earthly life had ended and their lives would never be the same, they knew Nathan was in Heaven and that one day they would see him again, because Nathan's faith in God and his relationship with Jesus was a certainty.

20

Earlier that evening back in Osawatomie after the football game had ended, the Osawatomie team came back to their locker room together, where Dave French and the other coaches met with their players and thanked them for their efforts during the season. At that time, they had no further information on the status of Nathan's injuries. Once the coaches concluded the meeting they went together as a group to watch the film of the night's game. It wasn't long after that when the Osawatomie athletic director came into the coaches' room and told them that Nathan was in surgery. Dave and the other coaches' worst fears had been confirmed, now knowing for certain the seriousness of Nathan's injuries.

Dave and the other coaches left the field house that night with Nathan's injuries weighing heavy on their minds. By the time Dave got home it was after midnight. Lori was still up, so Dave called his son Andy over and the three of them talked about Nathan. Dave told Lori and Andy that Nathan was in surgery and that he might not make it. Dave said he held his family as they cried together that night for Nathan. Dave said that he did not sleep at all that night for being concerned about what was transpiring at Kansas University Medical Center with Nathan and his family.

Across town Seth Jones was also up late. He too was trying to come to terms with his emotions. Seth had been at the front of the line that night when the Osawatomie team was leaving the locker room after halftime. He had a clear view of what was happening across the way on the Spring Hill side of the field. He had seen all the ambulances, the flashing red lights and the helicopter. Seth said to him it seemed almost unreal as he was watching everything unfolding. But being a teenager and playing in a ballgame no one really understood the gravity of the situation. Things like this don't happen in a football game.

Once the game was over Seth went back home and talked with a friend of his on his cell phone who was a student at Spring Hill High School. She had gone to the hospital where Nathan was taken and they stayed on the phone together until nearly four in the morning as she was giving him updates on what was happening with Nathan.

Seth said it was hard to sleep that night. His heart was racing with emotion. Seth had known Nathan for a long time, the two boys playing sports against each other for years. Seth and Nathan were not close friends, the two boys going to different schools, but he respected Nathan from competing against him in athletics, specifically football and basketball.

Nathan's close friend Eric Kahn, was not at the Osawatomie game that night. Eric and the Spring Hill soccer team were playing that night in the quarterfinals of the state soccer playoffs. That was the only game Eric had missed in his two years as a member of the Spring Hill football team.

Eric remembers that he and some of the other kids from the soccer team were eating at a restaurant after the soccer game when they got the news that Nathan had been injured. Eric says he and the other players were not that concerned when they first got the news that Nathan had been injured at the football game, because, as athletes, they realized that people get injured to some degree all the time playing football, and they assumed Nathan would be fine.

It was later when Eric and his friends on the soccer team realized how serious Nathan's injuries were.

"That was a scary situation for all of us and for a while after Nathan died it did not seem real. That was not something anyone our age is prepared for. I believe what happened to

Nathan made us all grow up faster, to see something like that happen to one of your friends."

Nic Madelen who was coaching on the sidelines for Spring Hill that night said that when Nathan went down on the sidelines everyone knew it was serious, but nobody thought at the time it would end like this.

"I think we were all concerned but you think he is going to be okay. After the game and on the way to the hospital we got more information and began to see how serious the situation was. No one thought it would be this bad.

"After Nathan died you begin to wonder if you want to keep coaching. You reevaluate what is important. Winning games and the score on the scoreboard become less important after experiencing something like this. It is a life-changing event on so many levels."

The Osawatomie game was the last time that group of Spring Hill football players were ever together as a team. Since it was the last game of the season, they did not practice or play together as a team again. At school Nic and the other coaches and players tried to go on. Nic said the coaches did their best to love on the kids and comfort them while they too were trying to grieve and process Nathan's passing themselves.

"We tried to keep going and give the kids a sense of normalcy after losing Nathan. We realized that we had to be strong for our players even though we were hurting too. We tried to keep things as normal as we could. We were trying to not live in fear. We wanted to set a good example for the kids, to show our students and athletes how to be strong in the face of adversity and deal with the hurts and struggles we all have to face during our lives in a positive supportive way.

"I think the experience of how Nathan lived his life, humbly, being kind to others, and the way his family responded to his death has been an inspiration to many of the young men who were on that team. Many of the players from that team have become fine young men, some of whom I am still in contact with today.

"The grace with which the family handled losing Nathan was amazing."

21

"The next day the confusion continued as the feeling that this can't really be happening lingered," Ron recalled.

"With brain injuries being such a hot topic especially in football, Nathan's story brought with it a lot of attention from the national news media. Along with all of the wonderful support our family received from people in our community there were also phone calls from national news media and others. Later in the day on Friday, as our home was full of caring friends, we received a phone call from Chris Nowinske who works with Dr. Ann McKee of the Bradford VA Clinic and Dr. Cantu of Boston. My friend Larry Sumner answered the phone and said they wanted to study Nathan's brain for the work they were doing on head injuries. At this point I leaned on Larry to help make the decision for me. Not sure what I told him, but we went along with their request."

In the weeks that followed, Dr. McKee and her team at Boston University found that Nathan had developed CTE. According to the Boston University CTE Center, Chronic Traumatic Encephalopathy (CTE) is a degenerative brain disease found in athletes, military veterans, and others with a history of repetitive brain trauma.

This diagnosis confirmed for the Stiles that there was no one to blame for what happened to Nathan. Nathan's injuries had developed over a long period of time and could not have been prevented.

22

Brian McCauley, who is the Editor/Publisher of the Miami County Newspaper, was tasked with the responsibility of covering the news story of Nathan's death for the local newspapers of Miami County. In addition to his responsibilities as Editor/Publisher for the local papers, Brian also found himself in the position of fielding requests from national news organizations that were inquiring information about Nathan.

With such an emotionally charged incident as was the case with Nathan's death, Brian and the other staff members of the local newspapers were responsible for reporting the news, which is their professional duty, while at the same time themselves experiencing the shock of Nathan's loss. Brian spoke about how the impact of Nathan's death rocked the Spring Hill community and impacted him personally.

"When you write for a small-town newspaper, it's nearly impossible to not be affected by the news you're covering in the community. Of course, you strive to be impartial and objective, but through the relationships you form with your sources you find yourself celebrating with them, worrying with them and grieving with them. Such was the case with my relationship with Miami County Commissioner, Ron Stiles. As a fellow Christian, I was inspired by the way Ron spoke openly about his faith. His son, Nathan, was no different. It's not every day you see a star athlete and homecoming king willing to plaster the words, 'Why live for anyone other than Jesus?' on his Facebook profile."

Brian recalls the emotions he felt when he received the news about Nathan. "I remember getting the call on Thursday night about what happened at the game, and my heart sank when I heard it was Nathan who collapsed. Once word of Nathan's death became public, it was like the entire Miami County community went into shock.

"I knew we had to cover what was happening from a news perspective, but I think we also felt like it was our responsibility to protect the Stiles family from other media outlets that might choose to sensationalize Nathan's death. At the time, there was a lot of national discussion about concussions as they relate to football, and Nathan's death quickly became a national news story. Because of that we never released any images of Nathan playing in that game.

"I remember the first time I called Ron following the incident. I dreaded the call. What do you tell a father who just lost his son? What meaningful question could I possibly ask him? I'll never forget how calm Ron seemed when I talked to him. It wasn't that he wasn't hurting, it was just that he was so secure in his faith that he was certain Nathan was in heaven with Jesus. Where many other parents would be searching for someone to blame for their son's death, Ron was very adamant that he wanted Nathan's story to be about Nathan's faith in God, not a story about concussions."

23

On Friday, October 29th, the day after the Osawatomie game, school was held as normal at Osawatomie High School and in Spring Hill. However, extra counselors were called in to both schools to speak with teachers, coaches and students as needed.

Dr. Wayne Burke, Superintendent of Spring Hill Schools, remembers, "Losing Nathan was devastating. Any time you lose a student, it is a tragedy. Losing someone so young can be the first experience with death for many students. When we lost Nathan the effect on our school community was widespread, because he had such a strong influence on so many lives. Many people in and outside the school district knew him either through school, sports, church, or within the community. They may not have questioned their own mortality before this, "but if it can happen to Nathan, it could happen to me." The school district reached out to other districts and asked them to send additional counselors to our schools, not just the high school, but in our other public schools as well. Nathan's passing not only affected our students, but also teachers, staff, and other adults throughout our community.

"Our goal was to be there to support the family and take care of the kids and staff. However, one question we knew we couldn't answer was why such a tragedy could happen? Many of us believe that had this event not happened Nathan would have gone on to college, married, and settled down to raise his family in the Spring Hill area. He would have had some type of leadership position in the community and continued to have a positive impact on many lives."

Katie George, guidance counselor at Spring Hill High School said, "The effect of Nathan's death was felt not just in the high school, but it rippled through the entire community. It still has an impact on our community today.

"The day that Nathan died was the most difficult day in my entire 20-year teaching career. We didn't do anything fancy to help students and colleagues that day. We simply hugged them, listened to them, and made our love and support for them known."

24

As the Friday school day progressed and the news about Nathan's death swept across the community, people began to ask questions. "How could something like this happen, and who was to blame?" With emotions running high, rumors started circulating that it was a tackle by one of the young men on the Osawatomie football team that caused Nathan's injury.

Seth Jones, the standout Osawatomie quarterback and safety had made a clean hard tackle on a Spring Hill ball carrier late in the first half of Thursday night's game. From the Osawatomie side of the field Seth's tackle occurred right in line with where Nathan was already down just off the playing field as he was being treated by medical personnel on the Spring Hill sideline.

That Friday morning at school a student came up to Seth and said something to Seth inferring that it was his tackle late in the first half that caused Nathan's accident. Seth knew that he was not responsible for what happened to Nathan, but still it was disturbing for Seth and all of the young men who were on the field that night to have been involved in a football game where one of the players from the opposing team had suffered a life ending injury. Seth's brother, Chad, was a teacher at the school that day, and after these rumors began to spread Seth went to Chad and told him what was being said and Seth then checked out of school and went home.

The next day on Saturday morning Seth was at home when he received an incoming call on his cell phone from a number he did not recognize. When Seth answered his phone the voice on the other end was Ron Stiles.

"I had received a concern that one of the players from the Osawatomie team was being blamed for Nathan's death. I reached out to find out if this was true. After speaking with Gary French, the Osawatomie School Superintendent, I found out it was," recalled Ron.

Gary French said that when he got the phone call from Ron asking how the students at Osawatomie were doing, and saying that he wanted to call Seth Jones, to tell him he was thinking about him, and that what happened to Nathan was no one's fault after losing his son, Gary could not believe it. "When I got the call from Ron, I was wondering what I would say to him. Then for Ron to tell me he was calling me to say that no one was to blame for what happened to Nathan, and he expressed concern for our students, and wanted to reach out to Seth, it was amazing."

Chad Jones, Seth's brother said, "For me personally it was almost unbelievable that someone that was going through what Ron was would take the time to call and talk to my brother, who I knew was hurting inside from what had occurred. I could tell it had a profound impact on Seth when Ron called him."

"I wanted Seth to know there was no way this was his fault, nor anyone's fault," Ron said. "Seth is a great young man from a great school, that has supported us from the beginning and we will always be grateful to them. I believed then, and I believe even more now, that this was an event that was going to happen no matter what we did."

The blur of events for the Stiles family continued as phone calls were made, visitors coming and going sharing their condolences, and plans for services being arranged. Still reeling from the previous day's events the Stiles family settled in at home, and as night fell the hectic day came to an end.

"As the story is told about the beginning of the Nathan Project, this is what brought us to that point," Ron said. "Later, on Saturday morning about 24 hours to the minute after Nathan died, Connie woke up talking about getting Bibles into the hands of youth, and how important it would be for everyone to have a Bible. How important it is for them to know Jesus. Hearing this gave me a bit of a smile and some sense of relief from all we were experiencing, as I could begin to feel the purpose in what God wanted us to do.

"As Saturday went on you could feel the birth of the Nathan Project, and begin to watch it grow.

"Later that day we were going to make Nathan's funeral arrangements. As I was getting ready to leave, I received a phone call from United States Senator Sam Brownback. He was calling to give us support and prayers for our loss of Nathan. This gave me a chance to tell him about the Nathan Project and the journey we were about to take. At the end of our talk he said, he had no idea our conversation would be such an inspiring one, and he prayed for us. Little did I know that this theme would continue, why? Because Jesus had his hand in it and we were just being his hands and feet.

"Going to the funeral home to plan Nathan's funeral was a hard thing to do. As I was getting ready to leave, I looked at the shoe rack and saw Nathan's shoes. After deciding to put them on I felt guilty because, was I really good enough to wear them? They were also bigger than my feet and I thought that my feet would never be big enough to fill them, but I can walk in them. In a strange way this gave me comfort.

"Towards the end of the day as we were sitting around the table at the funeral home Natalie received a text from Seth, the Osawatomie football player I had spoken with earlier that morning, saying he was glad that I had called him. We decided to set the visitation for November 2nd, which would have been Nathan's 18th birthday, the funeral and burial for November 3rd, and Nathan's Celebration of Life for November 4th.

"Once again, I felt God was leading me on this strange journey."

25

Spring Hill High School is a state-of-the-art facility which first opened to students in 2009. The building has large classrooms equipped with the most current technology. The athletic fields are the equivalent of those you would typically see at a small college or university. When you enter the main entrance of the building you are ushered through an expansive two-story glass foyer that leads from there to a large open hallway. After a short walk down the hallway and then turning to your right you are led through a pair of large double doors out onto a balcony that overlooks the gymnasium. Once you enter the gym's balcony you are standing some 30 plus feet above the gym floor. This is the gym where Nathan and the other members of the Spring Hill High School basketball team played their home games.

On November 4, 2010, just two days after what would have been Nathan's 18th birthday, the Stiles family held a Celebration of Life Service for Nathan in this gym. The gym had been rented for the service, as there was no other place in town that could accommodate the crowd of over 2500 people.

The Spring Hill Madrigals group, led by music director Georann Whitman, performed a choral arrangement to begin the service. This was the school's chorus group in which Nathan had been an active part for the previous four years. During that time Nathan had developed a strong bond with Mrs. Whitman and the other students in the group.

"I had Nathan in class for four years. He was very special to me. Nathan was very talented," Georann said. "He had a warm, rich baritone voice, but an even better ear for music. He was a leader in his section and in Madrigals - musically, socially and spiritually. When we lost him, the group didn't sound the same.

"Nathan and I never specifically spoke about how he felt about music, but there was really no need. Every time he sang, his face lit up. Music was inside of him. He was a very active participant in rehearsal - always wanting to get better personally, and for the group to do well. He almost never missed a single one of the many performances in the 3+ years he sang in my choirs - even with all of his other activities, which was a sign that music was an important part of who he was."

Pastor Joel Atwell, of Grace Community Church, was the first speaker to take the stage that night, and he began by thanking everyone for coming. As he looked across the gym floor lined with chairs and the gym seating filled with people he said, "On behalf of Nathan and his family, thank you all so, so much for being here tonight to celebrate the brief life and lasting legacy of Nathan Stiles. What an amazing tribute to Nathan and an encouragement to his family to have so many people come out tonight. What a beautiful testimony this is to the impact of his young life.

"Many of you are here tonight because you knew Nathan personally. You come tonight to honor a dear family member or a dear friend. Some of you perhaps had a less personal relationship with Nathan but you are here because of some connection to the family perhaps. Still others of you are here because you are a part of the larger community, or are a part of the larger fraternity of football fans who were touched by what happened to Nathan. But whatever your reason is for being here tonight, we just want to say thank you.

"At our church we believe very strongly in supporting others, we call this practice a ministry of presence. We believe that showing up matters; showing up matters, so thank you for being here tonight.

"As I have said we have come here tonight to remember Nathan and to mark Nathan's passing, and no doubt tonight there will be tears. It hurts to lose such a bright, vibrant young man. Nathan was a son, a brother, a grandson, nephew, and friend. It hurts to have a person like that ripped out of your heart. Nathan was my friend too. And I hate the fact that he is gone. So, if in this Celebration of Life Service there wasn't some sadness, there would be something wrong with us. However, that being said, we are coming together tonight to celebrate Nathan's life, a life well-lived.

"The question of why this happened has no doubt haunted each of us. Over these past few days there have doubtless been questions of why? But at some point, we have to move from asking "why" to "what now?" Perhaps tonight is that point, to move from "why" to "what now?" What do we do now?

"Along the way in this service tonight we are going to ask each of you to make what was one of the greatest passions of Nathan Stiles' life, his relationship with Christ, to become the one greatest passion of your life.

"We have no intentions of playing on your emotions tonight. We do not want you to make a shallow, hollow, spur of the moment decision. No, we are going to invite you to make an intentional, deliberate, thoughtful, prayerful, purposeful decision, a decision that has the power to completely change the direction and trajectory of your life, and the lives of those people around you for time and for eternity. So, buckle your chin straps, here we go."

Pastor Laurie Johnston, then came forward and stood at the podium. "These last couple of years, Nathan and I, and our youth group, have been talking about how can we get the Word of God into the schools? I never dreamed that I'd be up here tonight doing that very thing, thank you Nathan. This is

Nathan's Bible I have up here with me tonight," Laurie said as she held the Bible up in her left hand, "and he used it."

Paul Young was the next speaker, he was the first of three teachers that spoke that night.

"First of all, on behalf of the faculty and staff of our school and the entire district, Ron and Connie, we want to thank you for sharing your son with us. I think our entire faculty and staff would say that Nathan taught us more than we taught him. I had the privilege of being his history teacher and his Fellowship of Christian Athletes sponsor. What a dynamic person and impact Nathan made in our school!

"Also, Ron has been such a rock, and Connie an inspiration to everyone since this happened. Even though he is hurting, Ron is going around and loving on these kids here at school. Wow! Nathan would be so proud, and Connie, she was doing the same thing. I know Nathan must be up there in Heaven smiling.

"When I was asked to come here tonight and speak about Nathan, I thought to myself, 'How can I do justice to that kid? What will I say?' Then at our church service last Sunday, the preacher told a short story about serving others and it made me think of Nathan. The story goes like this. There was this grocery store and the owners were struggling a little bit. They were trying to think of new ways to connect with their customers. So, they asked each one of their employees to think of something that each of them could personally do well, what they could do best, to help the store to reach people, what could they do to make the customers feel special.

"There was this one young man who bagged groceries at the store, and he decided he would write a thought for the day and put it in each customer's bag he bagged groceries for, to let them know he cared about them. As time passed there would be lines of people who would come into the store to receive this young man's thought for the day. He knew how to make people feel special, and so did Nathan.

"So, I have written down some of what I think would be Nathan's thoughts if he were here to share them with you tonight. Some of the things Nathan did that were special, what Nathan did was contagious.

"One - You have to be involved to build a foundation for your faith. Two - Surround yourself with people who support you in your faith. Three - Keep your life pure for Jesus. Four - The greatest gift you can give your loved ones is for them to know without a doubt that you are going to heaven. Five - You don't need the alcohol, the drugs, the sex, the things of this world to be happy. Six - Love is contagious, and I got mine from Jesus. Seven - Why live for anyone other than Jesus?"

Rick O'Neil, Nathan's basketball coach was the next to speak. He described Nathan as a 'quiet leader.' Rick said that Nathan was not a boisterous type of person, that he never saw Nathan get upset with another player in practice or in a game when someone made a mistake. He was not the type of kid to cast blame on someone if the team lost a game, and when Nathan would make an error or turn the ball over, he would take the responsibility and try to do whatever he could to help the team. It was not uncommon to see Nathan go out of his way to help the younger players, leading by example with his work ethic, always giving 100% in everything he did.

Rick said, "Nathan was a coach's dream. I've coached a lot of years in a lot of different schools and school districts, and we have a lot of fine young men and young women in this school. We live in a great community. But of all the kids I have coached, Nathan would have to be in the top one percent. As a human being he was the kind of person we all would want to be associated with."

Brent Smitheran then took the stage and spoke about his memories of Nathan.

"Over the last three years I have had the honor and privilege to teach Nathan in two different math classes, and have coached him in basketball for three years. As a parent of a four-year-old boy, I hope and pray every night that my son grows up to be the man Nathan Stiles was. Nathan was the type of student that makes you want to be a teacher. When Nathan walked into your classroom, eyes bright, big toothy grin from ear to ear, you just could not help but feel better as a teacher about your day. He had the ability to draw people in, he made you a better person. The best way I could describe Nathan was that he was a giver of joy, because everywhere he went, he did his best to make people happy.

"On Friday many of our teachers were trying to help our students cope with the loss of Nathan, and while also trying to come to terms with what had happened ourselves, we gave the students opportunities to share some of their memories of Nathan. At the end of the day when the teachers came back together to reflect on the day's events, we shared with each other some of the comments we had heard throughout the day. Three of them really stuck with me this last week.

"There was one student in particular who had a class with Nathan who said, 'At the end of every class period he always wished me a great day, without exception.' Another student commented, 'Throughout all of his years going to school with Nathan, he looked up to Nathan because when things went wrong Nathan was always someone you could count on to step in and help support and shoulder the burdens of the other kids who were having a hard time at school.' Several of the teachers heard this comment that really spoke to me the most, 'Nathan Stiles was the only person at school who was always nice to me.'

"What is interesting about these comments was that many of them did not come from people who Nathan had strong personal ties with. They weren't upperclassmen he had gone to school with for many years, most of them were not members of the sports teams he played on, they were not necessarily members of his church group he had spent a lot of time with. There wasn't a common demographic there. The tie that brought all of those people together was that Nathan took the time to make people feel they were important. Because to Nathan, they were important, no matter what.

"You see, Nathan treated every person he encountered like they were his friend. If you were to survey the students here at Spring Hill High School, I would bet that there are at least 50 students here who felt like Nathan Stiles was their best friend.

"So, I have a challenge for the students, the next time you come to school, in one of your seven classes, I want you to make a heartfelt compliment to one of your classmates. When you are in the lunchroom or the hallway, I want you to say a simple hello to someone you would not normally speak to. In short, I want you to do just once tomorrow what Nathan did every day. Can you imagine what kind of a place Spring Hill High School would be, if everybody adopted Nathan's "pay it forward" attitude in life? Can you imagine how accepted and loved you would feel at school if we continued to treat each other that way?"

After Brent finished his remarks an emotional Natalie Stiles came forward and with her parents standing by her side she spoke about her brother.

"Nathan was the best big brother, and my best friend," Natalie said. "He was so good to me. He always protected me, and he cared so much about me. He loved me with all he had and was never afraid to show it. Whenever we got ready to go somewhere, he had to see what I was wearing so he would be dressed appropriately. Earlier this year on 'nerd day,' he asked me if we could match? So, we did; we had the best time together.

"And then on Thursday night, my whole world began to collapse," Natalie said, gently brushing away tears with her left hand as she bravely smiled, trying to regain her composure, Connie and Ron quietly stepping forward to stand closer by Natalie's side as she continued.

After speaking briefly about her sorrow Natalie professed that she knew Nathan was in Heaven, but still it was hurtful and confusing to lose her brother and best friend. But as the days had passed and she had seen the beginnings of the Nathan Project Ministry coming into place, she could see that Nathan's life and death did have meaning and purpose. She had seen God's purpose through the way Nathan had lived his life, and her faith in God's plan gave her hope.

Natalie spoke about how she and Nathan had done so many things together over the years. She spoke about how she and Nathan had talked about how they desired to change Spring Hill for God. "We had no idea at the time what God's plan was. But apparently God had a bigger plan for Nathan than what the world had to offer him."

She said that she and Nathan had decided that they refused to sit back and let one more day go by without giving all they had for the glory of God. Natalie declared, "God has given every person here tonight the chance to grow in their faith and to find purpose in God, and with a Savior as wonderful as that, "Why live for anyone other than Jesus?"

Connie Stiles took to the stage next wearing a yellow Spring Hill High School shirt and spoke from her heart about the loss of her son and the passion of Nathan's life, his love of God and his personal relationship with Jesus Christ. With remarkable composure and clarity, Connie articulately expressed her hopes for what was Nathan's dream; that more of his friends would come to know Christ.

"When I woke up Saturday morning," Connie said as she paused momentarily, then with passion resonating through her voice she professed, "I was on fire!" With the emotion of the moment sweeping across the crowd of onlookers she added, "I tell you what, I felt Nathan with me, he was with me and he was telling me, 'we've got to do something.' I knew Nathan loved Jesus. He made me a better person.

"So, on Saturday morning," Connie continued, "I ran away from home in my car. I went and saw my dad in the hospital. Then I went up to where I work, I just couldn't stay home. Then I went to meet with some of my dear friends at

Starbucks, and sat for two hours discussing the Nathan Project. We've got to do something to get Bibles into the hands of young people so that we can reach these kids for Jesus!"

Connie went on to say how when she and her friends were leaving Starbucks a man approached them in the parking lot that just so happened to be wearing a Youth for Christ hat and inquired about the score of the football game. Connie told him the score from the game and that her son Nathan had passed away after the game on Friday. To which the man said he was sorry, and asked Connie if there was anything, he could do for her? Connie then speaking to the crowd said, "But you know what, it was interesting, because we stood there together and talked for maybe twenty minutes, and he gave me his card and he said, 'If there is anything that Youth for Christ can do to help your project, you let me know.' Right then I knew, I knew this was going to work. I knew that Nathan's purpose was to bring people to Christ. The kids he loved so much, he'd come home and talk to me about some of his best friends who he was worried about, and he would ask me, 'what can we do?' and I would say pray for them.

"But Nathan, he had a purpose. God had a purpose for my Nathan, for our Nathan.

"The outpouring of generosity from this community has been unbelievable. You hear sometimes only about the bad in this world, but this is a good world.

"Nathan wanted his friends to be saved. And it's not just kids, parents too. Parents, if you don't know Jesus, how can you help your kids know Jesus? It takes commitment, but I can tell you it will be worth every second of your time to make sure your children know Christ. Because if it were your child who suddenly passes away, you need to know they know Jesus. God only knew it was Nathan's time, I had no idea; it was an ordinary day. Parents, please take the time to help your children know Jesus. Then one day when God calls for them you will know where they are going.

"There are 1000 Bibles back there with your name on them," Connie said as she pointed toward the tables in the back of the auditorium lined with Nathan Project Study Bibles.

"I want everyone here to have one. We never get too old to read the Bible. Because every time I read the Bible, I see something that jumps out at me that I didn't know before. So, I'm offering you, everyone here tonight, please, make a commitment to yourself and your family and take a Bible home with you. Along with the Bible, you need to sign up to participate in a one-year Bible study. You can't just take a Bible and sit it on the end table and expect to learn something. You have to open it up and read it for yourself. The Nathan Project, it isn't about this church or that church, it's about God.

"This is something that needs to be spread beyond Spring Hill. That is my desire and Nathan's desire, for everyone to know Jesus."

Moments later Ron, wearing a purple number '44' Spring Hill High School football jersey, stepped forward and took the microphone from Connie, and began to address the audience.

"First of all, we've talked an awful lot about Nathan tonight, and God loved him. Nathan had two wonderful brothers and sisters, and a mom that is on fire right now. I am so proud of her. My family is here, and that's wonderful. But what is so wonderful, as I look around, what a beautiful sight to see all of you here tonight. It is so awesome, and I thank you guys for being here tonight to help support our family. I just can't tell you how much that means to us. God bless you.

"A couple of things that I think need saying, just a few things that need to be said. This event was no one's fault. I had to make some calls over the last week, to talk to a few folks, to let them know that it was absolutely no one's fault. And I want you to hear that from us, please, loud and clear. It was just something that happened, it was a bad event, it hurt, but please, it was no one's fault. The other thing is that there has been a lot of talk about concussions. A lot of talk about what should have happened and what maybe should have been done different. All I can say, is if there is something that should be different, if something needs to be changed; it needs to be done with doctors, not lawyers.

"A lot of wonderful things have already been said tonight. I want to just leave you with a couple of thoughts. I wanted to ask, how many of you students have felt differently about your walk with God during this last week? Just raise your hands. It's made a change with me. I don't know why God has led me on this path, and my family on this path, but He is our God, and we are going to follow Him.

"The other thing I would like to talk about comes from the book of John, where Jesus asks a man who had been ill for many years, 'Do you want to get well? Do you want to get well?' You know all families have tragedies, and since this has happened, I have heard so many sad things, bad things. And it doesn't seem right that these things happen to people, and you have to wonder why? But Jesus asks all of us, 'Do you want to get well?' It's like Connie just talked about, you get in the Bible, you study the Word of God, and you follow Jesus, just like Nathan has told us to do, and when it comes time for you to meet the Lord, you will be well.

"We just want you all to be involved if you want to participate, take this opportunity tonight to take a Bible and sign up for a Bible study. If you're not well, get well.

"And I want to tell you kids something too, we have had some stories tonight, but this is just Nathan's dad talking to you, do just like coach Young told you all a while ago, it's important, to help each other out. You know, I have had so many of the younger kids tell me, especially the freshmen, 'You know Nathan, he was like a freshman, he treated us well," and that's so important. Guys, if you see a little kid out playing basketball somewhere, he needs someone to talk to him, say something positive to that kid, be compassionate, help him out a little bit. To the girls, be good to one another. I mean it is so nice to share kindness, and you will feel so good. I tell you what, you guys, all of you, were Nathan's buddies. You were his buddies; he loved you guys to death. So, thank you for that, God loves you, and God bless you."

Josie then came up to the podium and spoke about how she hoped that people would take the Bibles and make the time to read them for themselves so that they could decide on their own what they believed about God. She insisted that they not make a decision about who God is from what someone else had told them. "Read the Bible for yourself," she urged them. "So that you can see who God is."

When the time came for people to come forward and receive a free study Bible, Nathan's friends Mike Reynolds, Luke Johnston and Ian Johnston and the other members of the Awakening Band, that Nathan had co-founded, were on stage and they performed the song "Break In", a song that Nathan and Luke had co-written.

Mike confessed, "We were nervous. It was the first time we had played together as a group in front of people, and there were over 2500 people in the gym that night. But it was a service for Nathan and we were doing it for him. To look around and see everyone with their hands in the air in worship, it was amazing, being up on stage to see that was an unbelievable experience to say the least. We knew the Bibles would be there, but when Ron and Connie came up and spoke about the Nathan Project, whoa, what a legacy."

As the service was about to end, Connie returned to the stage and sang "Remember Me," by Mark Schultz, as a dedication to Nathan. As she began to sing, with her crystal-clear angelic voice filling the auditorium, the young people standing behind her on stage bowed their heads, and raised their hands in praise. Then people throughout the auditorium began to stand, with hands above their heads. What a moment.

"The Holy Spirit moving in the gym that night brought people to their feet with raised arms." Paul Young remembers, "It was an incredibly powerful moment to see God at work in such a tragedy. To see other kids/families being exposed to the opportunity for this comfort through the gift of the Bibles was awe-inspiring."

"Ron and Connie Stile's faith was amazing. From day one they were kind and generous, even in their loss they were giving. Their attitude of giving glory to God in the midst of their loss was an encouragement to other believers in our community and still is today," recalled Dr. Jeff Dorsett.

Travis Bosse and Nicole VanDaele were sitting in the crowd that night along with Nicole's mother, father and younger brother Jake. They were sitting on the north side of the gym towards the top of the lower level of bleachers. When the time came for the Bibles to be given away Nicole and Jake came forward and received their Bibles.

After the service ended, ESPN reporter Wayne Drehs made his way down to the gym floor to meet with Ron and Connie. Wayne, who was sent to Spring Hill to write a story for ESPN Magazine, asked Ron if he and Connie would be willing to go on air, to tell their story on television for an *Outside the Lines* documentary.

"We were not too wild about the idea at first. We did not want to turn this into a culture media event," revealed Ron. "However, when Wayne made the point of how doing the documentary would help others learn about Nathan's story, which is about Jesus, and how important it would be to share that message with as many people as possible, plus he would also come back to help film the documentary, we agreed to do it.

"As Wayne and I finished speaking about happiness and the subject of taking this to court, I finally asked him what he would do. He talked about the damage that could be created by filing a law suit and I said, 'Exactly.' We drove that message from the funeral on. If something needs to be learned from this it should be from doctors not lawyers."

Later, as Ron and Connie were speaking with some of the people who had attended the ceremony, Seth Jones, the Osawatomie football player that Ron had called to check on the Saturday morning after the Osawatomie game, came up to Ron and introduced himself. Seth thanked Ron again for calling him, and Ron gave Seth a yellow and purple Nathan Project memorial wrist band.

"I have worn one of those Nathan Project wrist bands Ron gave me ever since that day," Seth proclaimed. "You can even see it in my wedding pictures."

26

Hillsdale Presbyterian Church is located in the farming community of Hillsdale, Kansas, just a short 10-minute ride from Spring Hill. The church was founded 150 years ago, shortly after the end of the Civil War. It was in 1866 that A.M. Wilson organized the Mount Zion Presbyterian Church in a settlement about two miles west of the church's present location.

In 1872, a small tract of land was purchased in Hillsdale for $50.00. A year later the Mount Zion congregation voted to move to Hillsdale and renamed the church Hillsdale Cumberland Presbyterian Church. The original church building was built in 1873 and still stands today.

It is a beautifully maintained historic building with stained-glass windows and a bell tower. In 2005, the church added a new 6,200 square foot multi-purpose building, and in 2016, the growing congregation of 200, built a new sanctuary, connecting the old sanctuary and the multi-purpose building together.

Shortly after the Celebration of Life Service for Nathan on a Sunday morning, Wayne Drehs and Tom Quinn representing ESPN, showed up at the Stiles home to go to church with them. As they arrived at Hillsdale Presbyterian Church, the ESPN film crews were already there preparing to film the service, which created quite a buzz among the congregation who were arriving for church.

"Pastor Laurie said that a lot of the folks were upset as they felt the ESPN crew would be disturbing church." Ron continues, "I told her I would speak at the beginning of the service to explain to the congregation why they were there. I told the members of the congregation that, 'ESPN is looking for the story on who Nathan was, and what he was about. We thought there was no better place than Nathan's church to answer these questions.' Not only did that calm the rest of the service, but the ESPN film crew was holding hands with the congregation at the end.

"Once the church service ended, we went back to our house with all kinds of food waiting for us and finished filming the story, it aired on November 28th. We will always appreciate ESPN for doing this story on Nathan's life, and cherish the friendships we made with them."

27

The cheers of 60,000 fans disappeared in an instant, along with a young man's dream of playing football in the NFL. It was a Saturday afternoon October 23, 2010 in Stillwater, Oklahoma, the 14th ranked Oklahoma State University football team was playing host to the 16th ranked University of Nebraska. Andrew Hudson had recently been cleared to play football again after recovering from back surgery, and he was eager to suit up for this highly anticipated nationally televised game. However, due to his lengthy rehab from his back surgery he was underweight for the defensive line, and his coaches decided to utilize his speed on the kickoff. While running down on the kickoff team he suffered a concussion from a helmet to helmet hit. The offending player was suspended for one game for the illegal hit, but Andrew would never play football again. It took weeks for his memory to return, and he was forced to drop out of school for the remainder of the semester.

When Andrew returned to college, he stopped by the training room to see the athletic trainers that he had gotten to know so well throughout his many injuries at OSU. One member of the training staff approached Andrew and handed him an article about Nathan Stiles. The trainer told Andrew that he saw many similarities between him and Nathan, and advised Andrew to read the article. Andrew reports it was as if he was reading an article written about himself as it described a young Christian man who was outspoken about his faith, kind to everyone he encountered, and how he had a football related head injury the same week that Andrew suffered his concussion. Andrew wasn't sure what he needed to do, but he felt led to reach out to this family in some form or fashion.

Andrew's injury and the intervention of the Oklahoma State trainer began a chain of events that Ron describes as, "One of the most powerful 'only God could do' things that has happened to us on our journey with the Nathan Project."

* * *

Shortly after the Stiles family began the Nathan Project, they started a Facebook page. On November 19th, Ron was contacted on Facebook by a man from Amarillo, Texas. The man shared that he was touched by Nathan's story in part because his faith had been tested too after experiencing the loss of a close friend. He went on to tell Ron that, "The faith your family has shown from the moment this happened to Nathan is truly an inspiration to me."

This man, who Ron had never met, then said that he would like to put Ron in contact with a friend of his named Warren who had an ESPN Radio show in the Amarillo area called, *My Passion is Football*. The man went on to say that after reading Nathan's story he had called Warren and told him about their story and he asked Warren if he would be interested in having Ron and Connie on the show to speak about Nathan and the Nathan Project. Warren said he would be honored.

"Our passion was not football", Ron said, "but for some reason it seemed important to do the interview, so we went ahead and did the phone broadcast with Warren.

"At this point we had not yet filmed the *Outside the Lines* interview with ESPN so we thought this might help us get prepared for that. The radio interview was fairly uneventful, head injuries and the whole gamut of do's and don'ts regarding football injuries. We were thinking after the interview aired, we might have lots of requests from people wanting Bibles. But nothing much came from it, or so we thought."

Later, on December 2, 2010, Ron was contacted on social media by a college football player named Andrew Hudson. This young man wrote "that he was a redshirt freshman football player at Oklahoma State, who was desperately in love with Jesus, and he felt led by God to reach out to him."

You see, the Nathan Stiles article given to Andrew detailed Nathan's kindness towards others, and how Ron, his dad, started a Facebook page in case people needed someone to talk to in his son's absence. Andrew remembers being unsure what to say as he typed out a simple message informing Ron of who he was, and how he felt God calling him to reach out. Andrew remembers feeling apprehensive to reach out to a grieving father that he had never met, in a state he had never been to, to start a conversation that he didn't know the purpose of. However, Andrew was obedient to the conviction that he felt the Lord lay on his heart, and he reached out to Ron.

Ron replied, "I can sure call you. I think you sound like a special guy."

"Thank you, sir, I really appreciate that, but if you have any time to talk, I would like to come and talk with you in person. I wouldn't be opposed to driving up to Kansas from Oklahoma." Andrew was grateful for Ron's willingness to talk, but he felt the Lord calling him to go see his family, and thus he pushed the conversation rather quickly to ask if Ron would allow him to visit them.

Ron told Andrew if he wanted to come to Kansas, they would be happy to have him and, "That Connie could really use a hug right now, and if you could come up here and give her a big hug I think that would be worth the whole trip."

After a handful of Facebook messages back and forth, and one quick phone call, early in December on a Saturday morning Andrew Hudson arrived at the Stiles' house.

Ron said, "It didn't take us long to find out that Andrew was not really good with directions, but when he got here it was like we had known him all of our lives. He sat on the couch telling us about his life and his strong commitment to Jesus. We could see a lot of similarities to Nathan as we continued our talk."

Later that day they ended up at the local grocery store where they just so happened to be having free sample day. Andrew being very tall stuck out in the crowd. "With his smile and personality," Ron said, "he started conversations with not only our friends but other folks who we had never met. I had some people come up to me and ask, 'Who is this guy? Is he a relative? No? How long have you known him?' To the last question I looked at the time and said, 'About three hours!' With a smile."

As they were leaving the store getting ready to check out, Andrew struck up a conversation with the cashier, and when he learned of the difficult day, she was having he bought her a simple gift from alongside the checkout aisle, hoping it would brighten her day.

Ron returned to the store later that evening and the young lady at the checkout counter asked him, "Who is that guy?" She told Ron she had been having a tough time lately, and how much it meant to her that someone would care enough to do such a kind thing for her. She had been having a bad day, but that all changed when Andrew showed up.

"It was like Andrew was sent by God to help us through a very rough time," Ron declared. "We found out he had packed a bag and was ready to spend the weekend with us and that is what he did." That day Andrew attended a Fellowship of Christian Athletes event that was held in the community, spent time with several of Nathan's close friends, and more importantly spent time with Natalie to listen to and love on a sister who desperately missed her brother. Supernaturally Andrew quickly became integrated into their family, and he was able to hug a mother who longed to hug her son again, cry with a sister who longed to laugh with her brother again, and speak with a father who craved to hold and talk with his son again. Not only did God use Andrew in the lives of the Stiles family, but their family was instrumental in Andrew's life as well. It gave Andrew solace to see how the abrupt end to his football career could bring God glory, and could so intimately love on a family in such desperate need. Andrew had peace with his football career ending, and forever could look back to the Stiles family as a reminder of how good God is, and how He uses everything for the good of those who love Him, to those called according to His purpose.

Before Andrew returned to Stillwater, he remembered one last detail he left out, "Mr. Ron, I forgot to tell you that while I was on my way to see you, I received a call from Warren."

"Warren, I asked?" said Ron.

"Did you and Connie do a radio show with him?" ask Andrew.

"My mind flashed back to that radio interview that I thought had been a waste of time," Ron recalled, "and I said 'yes, we did do an interview with Warren.'"

Warren had called Andrew, prior to his trip to see the Stiles, to ask Andrew if he was going home to Bushland, Texas that weekend. Andrew told him that instead of going to Bushland, he was traveling to Kansas to see the Stiles family, and Andrew asked Warren if he had heard of Nathan's story? To Andrew's surprise, Warren said yes, and informed Andrew that he had interviewed the Stiles family just a week and a half earlier.

"Turns out Bushland is only ten minutes away from Amarillo, and Warren was one of the men who helped prepare Andrew for college football. It gave me chills to think about how through a Facebook post we connected with a man we had never met, who after hearing our story asked us to do a radio interview, that at the time we thought was not important, with a different man, who ended up being an integral figure in the life of a young man who showed up at our doorstep after his athletic trainer told him about Nathan. I knew God had to have had His hand in making all of this work," exclaimed Ron.

"From that weekend on Andrew was and is a part of our family."

Once Andrew returned to Stillwater he wrestled for a period of time as to whether or not to continue playing college football. As time passed Andrew made the decision to not return to the football team.

"Andrew is a very gifted athlete, so he went from playing college football to throwing the discus on the Oklahoma State track team and we went to see him in a track meet at the University of Oklahoma." Ron continued, "The next event we went to see Andrew participate in was at the Kansas University Relays which were held close to Spring Hill. When we got there Andrew said he had met a reporter while on the treadmill at the hotel from *The Lawrence Journal*. Andrew told the reporter about our story and he wanted to meet us. So, we met that day and the reporter was talking about Andrew and how his story with us was inspiring and how interwoven our two stories had become. I asked him if he had watched the *Outside the Lines* story on Nathan? He said no, and then he asked me if a certain ESPN reporter had done the story? I told him it was a reporter named Tom Quinn. I knew from the look on his face something was up. I asked, 'You know Tom, don't you?' He said yes, and then he proceeded to tell me how Tom had made a huge difference in his life.

"Imagine that, I thought," said Ron.

"Sometime later we traveled to Dallas and went to Andrew's wedding," Ron recalled. "He is married now with a beautiful wife and a young son. Andrew recently graduated from medical school and is completing a residency in dermatology. I am sure he is going to be a great physician."

Natalie told us later that she had prayed for God to send someone to help us after Nathan died. Our prayers were answered by a young man named Andrew."

Andrew was an answer to prayer. Andrew admitted, "He felt God had sent him to Spring Hill to meet the Stiles, and that he prayed as he was driving to Spring Hill that, he could be God's hands and feet to help bring healing to the Stiles family."

As both the Stiles family and Andrew reflect on the first weekend they met and all the life that has passed since then, they are unable to take credit for anything, but instead are left in awe of God's love and mercy, and how brilliantly He can use all things to bring Himself glory and how He can love on His people through the body of Christ.

28

Mike Reynolds was there in the waiting room with Nathan's family and friends at the hospital the night Nathan died. Earlier that day Mike says he and the other members of the Awakening Band had been in a recording studio working on a song, "Break In," that Nathan co-wrote with Luke Johnston. "That evening Ian Johnston, Luke's younger brother, was singing the lead vocal for the first time, the position Nathan held before leaving the band to play football his senior year," says Mike.

Just a few days later the Awakening band would be on stage performing "Break In" at Nathan's Celebration of Life Service.

Mike remembers the gymnasium that night was packed, standing room only. From Mike's position on stage he could see all that was transpiring and the emotion on the faces of the people in the attendance. "It was amazing. I have never seen anything like that before and I don't know that I will ever see anything like it again. The Holy Spirit was at work in that place. There is no denying it. It was an incredible moment.

"When Nathan died, I was in junior college going to culinary school," Mike continues, "and for a long time after that I really struggled with Nathan's death. I felt lost for a while after Nathan died."

Mike said it seemed impossible to believe that his friend Nathan could have died so suddenly, and he like many of Nathan's other friends were not sure how to handle what they were feeling. Then, a few months later one night on his way home from a night class, Mike got caught in a snow storm and he wasn't sure if he would make it home, so he called on Ron for help.

"I was still a student at Johnston County Community College in culinary school at the time, and I was driving home one night when I got caught up in a really severe snow storm. The weather conditions turned what would normally be a thirty-minute drive into about a two-hour trip. As I was driving along, I started to have some car trouble and I called Ron and told him, 'I don't think I can make it home.' So, Ron told me to stop at his house on the way home that night and I did. I spent the night at their house.

"I made it home the next day and when I did, I called Ron to let him know I had made it home safely, but that I thought I was having some pretty serious mechanical problems with my car. It was about two weeks later when Ron called me and asked me to come over to his house and talk. When I got there Ron told me that he and Connie had been talking and they thought, 'It's time to see Nathan's car back on the road,' and they wanted to give me Nathan's car."

A few days later Mike says his grandmother drove him over to the Spring Hill Oil Station where Ron had cleaned Nathan's car up and had the oil changed. When Mike walked inside Ron tossed Mike the keys. Ron had already taken care of the title work so the car became a free gift to Mike.

For the next five years Mike drove Nathan's car. During those years Mike says he put over 180,000 miles on Nathan's car. Mike declared, "Whenever I was in that car I felt like Nathan and I were riding together. I felt like I was riding with my best friend again.

"When I bought my first car myself, I paid $400 for it, and then my father and I worked on it together to get it up and running. The Stiles family probably does not know this, but when they blessed me by giving me Nathan's car, I was able to bless another friend of mine by being able to gift my old car to him. I was able to bless him with my car, because they blessed me.

"It was an emotional experience for me years later when it came time for me to get another vehicle and replace Nathan's car. Receiving the Stiles family gift of Nathan's car was very special to me."

Sometime later Mike began to sense that God was calling him into the ministry to become a youth pastor. But he wasn't sure what to do about it or how he would pay for school.

Then out of the blue one day, Mike got a call from someone who was affiliated with the junior college where he was attending culinary school, and they told him they were contacting him to see if he would be interested in transferring over into the ministry program at the school.

"I couldn't believe it," Mike exclaimed.

The school offered Mike a scholarship to pay his tuition. This solidified to Mike, that God was indeed calling him into the ministry to be a youth pastor.

Mike is currently serving as the youth pastor at Hillsdale Presbyterian Church.

29

A few weeks after Nathan died some of the kids in Nathan's Sunday school class at Hillsdale asked Loree Heiber if they could talk about their feelings, the sadness they were experiencing after losing Nathan. At the meeting Loree asked the teens in the class to choose one word that best described Nathan to them. One of the words the teens used to describe Nathan was 'faith.'

Loree told the teenagers that 'faith makes everything possible but not necessarily easy, and Nathan worked hard at his faith.' Loree says the words the teenagers chose that day truly reflected the person Nathan was.

"When it came time for our closing, we stood in our usual circle of prayer holding hands, and these beautiful, sincere prayers went up from the teenagers. As they went around the circle in order, the young people spoke of thankfulness to God for Nathan being in their lives. They shared their prayer concerns for his family, and asked that God would grant strength to all of us who knew Nathan and were touched by his life."

As the teens went around the circle each saying their prayers it came time for one young man in the group to pray. When he began to speak, Loree could see that he was struggling with his emotions; through his sadness and tears he couldn't speak. Loree told the group, "That God hears these types of unspoken prayers," and they went on to the next person in the circle. Later, when they were about to close, this young man said, 'I have to pray this prayer,' and slowly he got these words out.

"Dear Lord, I just want to pray what it seemed Nathan prayed in this room every Sunday. 'That we will go out and walk in your path and make a difference in our school.' Lord, many of us have prayed that prayer in this room – but Nathan truly did it – I don't think any of us can say it as well as he did, but help us to follow in his footsteps anyway."

"Nathan truly lived his life this way," Loree told the group, "by reading his Bible every day and asking God for help in how he lived. I think God would want me to say this to all of you kids – children and teenagers. You all have wonderful talents God has given you. You are all special in God's eyes.

"Yes, Nathan was a good teacher to all young and old. He truly was the words his Sunday school class used to describe him.

"Kind – Positive – Amazing – Loyal – Mentor – Beautiful – Uplifting

"Hard Working – Inspirational – Trustworthy – Warm Hearted – Humble

"He was all these and more," Loree proclaimed. "Nathan's life, though short, was full. Thank you, God for Nathan Stiles, whom we love with all our hearts."

Part 2

30

Shortly after the Nathan Project began, Doug Atteberry and the pastoral team at Grace Community Church started one of the Nathan Project Bible studies where they quickly had about a hundred kids showing up at church for Bible study. Doug says the church was initially gifted several cases of the New Living Translation Study Bibles by the Nathan Project.

"One of the things that everyone agreed on immediately," Doug remembers, "was how much the students attending the Nathan Project Bible study at our church liked the format of the New Living Translation Bibles."

It was during this time that Doug was taking some ministry classes working toward his pastoral degree and met Todd Miller, who was also attending seminary classes. The two soon became good friends. A few weeks later during the course of one of their conversations Todd told Doug that he was going into the juvenile correction facilities and leading a Bible study, and that in the facility they were using King James Bibles. Todd told Doug that many of the kids in the facility who were using the King James version Bibles did not understand what they were reading. Doug immediately thought of the Nathan Project.

"I thought to myself, I need to get him in contact with Ron," Doug continues, "and get some of the Nathan Project Bibles in his hands. So, I contacted Ron and told him, 'Hey I met this guy who goes to seminary classes with me who I want you to meet. He is going into juvenile correctional facilities and doing Bible studies, and it would be a great opportunity for us to get the Bibles into these facilities.' So, the two of them met and once Todd met Ron, it kind of went from there. Over the years they have been able to get Bibles into drug rehab and detention centers, prisons, county jails, and it has grown and grown and grown over the years."

"When I first met Ron, I was going to school working toward being ordained into the ministry, and I was also the founder and CEO of Shepherds Care Ministries," Todd recalls. "Along with that, I was a volunteer chaplain at a juvenile detention center in Olathe, Kansas. Doug and I were in a ministry class together, and one day he asked if I needed any Bibles for our Bible studies at the correctional facility. We had Bibles, but they were the King James version and they were difficult for the kids to read and understand. I was excited when Doug told me that he had a resource who would give us New Living Translation Study Bibles, because I knew they would be a better resource for the kids we were ministering to. He proceeded to tell me the story of Nathan Stiles, and how the Nathan Project Ministry began, and he asked me if I would be interested in talking to Ron.

"Up until that time the facility where I was leading the Bibles study had been using about 30 Bibles a year to give to the kids in the facility. When I told Ron how many Bibles I needed, he immediately gave us a couple of cases of Bibles, and there are 18 Bibles in a case. I was very excited to have what I thought would be a year's supply of Bibles.

"Once I got the Bibles from Ron the staff at the facility said they would take the Bibles around to the kids in the facility and give them to anyone who wanted one. At that time, we had between 60 and 70 kids housed in the facility. Within an hour of delivering the Bibles, I got a call back from the staff at the facility saying that they had given all of the Nathan Project Study Bibles away and they needed more Bibles. I told Doug we needed more Bibles and within a few days, more Bibles were delivered to the facility courtesy of Ron and the Nathan Project.

"I am not sure if the facility requesting more Bibles so quickly is what stirred Ron's curiosity or what, but I got a message from Doug asking if I would be interested in meeting and talking with Ron about what we were doing with our ministry in the facility. So, we met, and immediately I fell in love with the Stiles family. Once I met with Ron and heard the message that Ron was presenting of the Gospel, the way he was presenting God's Word, we asked him if he would present the story of Nathan's life there at the facility.

"The staff there at the facility was excited to have Ron come and speak to the kids. But at the same time, to put 60 or 70 kids in a room together at one time in a detention center facility, kids who are having trouble with the law, in one large open room together for security purposes was a concern. But we knew it was important for the kids to hear Nathan's story and to learn more about where the Bibles came from. Sure enough, God opened the door for us to get the 60 or 70 some odd young men and women there together in the gymnasium at the facility. Both Ron and Connie came that day, and shared the Gospel message from their heart, and told Nathan's story, and the mission of the Nathan Project. They had stacks and stacks of the Nathan Project Bibles there. When they finished speaking there wasn't a dry eye in the house, including staff.

"The staff came to me later and told me they had never seen the kids in the facility, the incarcerated youth, behave like that before. They were so well-behaved, they were attentive, they paid attention. Every one of them was tearing up. It was very moving for them. The staff was touched too by what Ron and Connie shared that day; it really took hold of everybody in that gymnasium. We knew then that God was on track to do something quite amazing with the Nathan Project," exclaimed Todd.

Soon after that, Ron started coming to the facility with Todd for the Bible studies. At first, Ron and Todd held Sunday services at three different facilities in Johnston County Kansas, and Todd says Ron would consistently come to every one of those facilities. Before long, Todd was being asked by the Adolescent Facility for Drug Treatment in Johnston County to come and provide chaplaincy there too, and Ron came with him, as Todd would say, "The Nathan Project went with us everywhere.

"For several years now," Todd continued, "Ron and the Nathan Project have been supportive of several different organizations that have been ministering to incarcerated people in various correctional facilities and drug rehab centers across the state of Kansas. In these facilities where we were ministering, we saw a dramatic difference when working with the youth who were struggling to read and understand the language in the King James Bibles, and then seeing them begin to take hold of what they were reading in the New Living Translation Study Bibles provided by the Nathan Project. It was amazing to see how big of a difference it made in the youth once they were reading Bibles written in a language that they could understand. This New Living Translation Study Bible was written with inserts that related to teenagers, and it really helped them to better learn and understand God's Word."

At some of the facilities, parents and family members were also allowed to come to the church services on Sundays and spend time with their loved ones. Todd says to have a kid's mom come up to you and see tears streaming down her face thanking them for reaching out to her troubled youth and getting her child into reading the Bible was very moving for everyone involved.

"They couldn't believe the change they were seeing in these kids who were now reading the Bible," Todd declared. "The parents, the grandparents, brothers and sisters were seeing these remarkable transformations in their youth who were attending the Bible studies. By reading their Bibles many of these young people were being transformed by the message of the Gospel.

"Over time we even began to see instances where the youth were ministering to their families. God began using these young people, who were put into a place where the Nathan Project was providing Bibles to them. Once they received God's Word and began to read it, they then began to minister to and change the lives of their whole family."

Whenever one of the youths they were ministering to would be released to go home, Todd says they always took the Nathan Project Bible with them. There were also times when kids would age out of the detention centers and be transferred to an adult facility. Over the years Ron and Todd began to go to the adult facilities and visit some of them too, and once they did, they were given the green light to come into the adult facilities and gift away Bibles in those facilities as well. Then from there, the Bibles began to be sent to youth and adult facilities across the state of Kansas and then on to other states as well.

"Since the Nathan Project began gifting Bibles in the correctional facilities there have been many times I would go up and visit inmates in the state facility," said Todd. "Whenever I would go to one of these facilities, the officers would come up to the front where I entered and they would bring me inside and walk me back to visit the pods where some of the young people that I was ministering to were housed.

'There was this one young man who came from a gang lifestyle," Todd continues, "and over the time he was in the facility and we had been ministering to him, he had been very positively affected by reading and studying his Bible. But still, this young man knew he had time to do as a result of the past offenses he had committed. He realized he still had to pay the consequences for what he had done.

"So, as I am walking through the facility to meet him, I hear this hollering and all of this noise and commotion going on inside the correctional facility, and I am thinking, '*What is going on in here?*' To be honest with you, I was a little nervous. But the officer who was escorting me didn't seem to be concerned at all, which made me feel better. Then as we got into the doorway, the glass doorway that leads into the pod, I see this young man, my friend who I had been working with, he had been let out of his cell and he was walking around outside the other cells holding up his Nathan Project Bible. This young man was yelling out scripture at the top of his lungs. He would then stop and put his ear up to one of the cell doors, and then you would hear the other person who was inside the cell scream back scripture from inside the cell. Then he would smile and go to the next cell and yell out another scripture, not even opening up his Bible, just yelling out scripture from memory. It became a sort of contest where one person would quote a scripture God had given them that day from their Bible Study, and then another person would quote a scripture that had spoken to them from their daily study.

"What a huge blessing it was for me to stand there and witness that," proclaimed Todd. "I told the officer, 'Don't interrupt, just let it go on.' Then later once the youth realized I was there I entered the pod and told them how proud I was of them. Afterwards we sat down in the facility around a metal table and talked about God's Word.

"There are many, many stories of young people who have had their lives changed by the Nathan Project Bibles and the Bible studies. One young lady who was in the youth facility, whenever I would be teaching, without fail, she would ask questions. She would always raise her hand right in the middle of a lesson and she would ask a question about what we had been talking about. It got to the point where some of the kids in the group would say to her, 'Just stop asking the pastor questions so he can finish the lesson.' I kind of chuckled and said, 'No, I want you guys to ask questions, this is the time where I want you guys to ask questions so you can learn.' So, this girl continued to consistently ask questions. One day I took this girl aside and I told her 'you are asking a lot of questions, and they are a lot of great questions, but some of these questions I cannot answer. But the scripture tells us that

He will reveal the answers to us, that God will reveal Himself to us if we study and continue to seek Him. He will reveal the answers to many of these questions to your heart.'

"As time went on, she was released to go back home to her family, and once she left the facility, she was able to take her Nathan Project Study Bible with her. A few weeks later I heard from this girl and she told me, 'Pastor, you won't believe what happened to me. You told me that God would reveal himself to me, like it says in His Word. He has done that. I understand more and more every day. The more I am reading His Word, the more I understand, and He is lifting me up, He is revealing Himself to me as I read my Bible.'

"She then went on to tell me that since her family had seen how much the Bible had done in her life, her whole family wanted a Bible. 'How can I get more of these Bibles,' she asked? Again, Ron was there. We took over a half a dozen or a dozen or so Bibles to that young lady and she started holding a Bible study in her apartment for anyone in her apartment complex that wanted to come.

"It is just amazing what is going on through the Nathan Project and the sharing of God's Word. We couldn't thank the Nathan Project enough for the impact it has made.

"We had another ministry," Todd revealed, "called Shepherds Care, where we gave single moms a place to live for free for two years in our apartment complex. It was called the Beadle Complex. Some of these young ladies came from some really bad places."

One of the requirements to participate in Shepherds Care Ministry and receive the free housing, was the participants had to attend church somewhere. Once they were accepted into the program if they did not already have a church home, Todd would help them find a church. In addition to being in church, they also had to attend a Bible study held there at the facility. They also had to either have a job or be enrolled in school full time, or a combination of work and school. They had some requirements they had to complete, but as long as they met those requirements, Todd says their rent and utilities were free for two years.

"Probably 80 percent of them had never been exposed to the Bible before," Todd remembers. "They would show up and the first thing we would do would be to give them a Bible donated by the Nathan Project. And then to see the changes in them, and their little boys and girls, the changes God was making in their lives as they were studying their Bibles was incredible. Being exposed to God's Word, and being in the presence of Christian people who were working to help them, and enjoying life, it was life changing for many of these women and their families. Many of these women and their families, over time were able to move out on their own, some of them bought homes, others were married, and some still attend the churches that we brought them into when they first entered the program. For these women and their families, studying the Bible was breaking chains, changing the cycles that they had been stuck in.

"These Nathan Project Bibles have not just been given to the incarcerated youth or adults; they have also been given to single moms throughout our Shepherds Care programs. Any new member who attends the church that I pastor today is given a free study Bible, donated by the Nathan Project. These Bibles have been given away to many people in many places, and the Bibles have been life changing, life altering.

"But the Bible itself, it doesn't do you any good unless you open it up and read it," declares Todd. "You don't read the Bible like a text book; you read it like a love story, God's love story to us. And that is one of the things that I really truly love about the Nathan Project. They have not only given away these Bibles for free, and they have given away thousands and thousands of them all over the world, but they also go, and they teach, they answer questions; they do life with people. Ron is always quick to start a Bible study, anywhere, anytime, that he has the time. And to this day, Ron is still faithfully volunteering in these facilities, years and years later, spending his time in youth facilities and adult facilities sharing the message of the Gospel.

"God placed upon Ron's heart to not only give the Bibles away, but to help people open them up, and to help people read it, and to help people understand it. That commitment, to teaching and volunteering, helping get the Bibles into people's hands, and working with them to help them read and understand God's Word, is a huge part of the Nathan Project mission," proclaimed Todd.

Doug Atteberry now pastors a church in Lincoln, Nebraska. In that church Doug says, "God has opened up the door for us to do some prison ministry here as well. In fact, we now have a number of inmates from the adult prison system in our area that attend our church on a weekly basis. Since our move to Nebraska, Ron has sent several cases of the Nathan Project Bibles to us, so every inmate that comes to our Bible study, we are able to provide a free Nathan Project Bible to them. That ministry is growing now to the point where we are beginning to launch several Bible studies inside these facilities. And of course, we are going to use the Nathan Project Bibles for these studies as well.

"These New Living Translation Bibles are such a great Bible for people who have never studied the Bible before," says Doug, "and the story that is written in the front and back covers of the Bible, Nathan's story, is very impactful as people reading the Bibles come to know Nathan's story as well.

"In the beginning we started with one youth facility, and from there the Nathan Project has spread to other facilities throughout our state, and then to other states across the United States. Over the years those Nathan Project Bibles have been given to people in various places around the world.

"Over the years it has really been cool to see how God has taken the heart that Ron and Connie had to get Bibles into the hands of as many people as possible, and to really see that happen. And today to know that tens of thousands of the

Nathan Project Study Bibles have been given away through their faithfulness is truly amazing.

"In addition to what has already happened with the Nathan Project, something new we are working on right now is that we have some friends who are missionaries in the Philippines, and God has really given them a lot of favor in that country. The school systems there have actually opened up for them to be able to go in and do discipleship training in the public schools. They have a great teaching curriculum, but one of the things they have been in need of is Bibles. They'll go into a city in the Philippines and they'll have 15,000 to 20,000 students that they are able to do discipleship training with but they need Bibles. One of the things we are praying about right now, is to find ways to provide them with Nathan Project Study Bibles. We want to help these missionaries, to get them Bibles to use in their mission work in the Philippines, to put Bibles in the hands of these people who desperately need and want them."

31

"Our kids played little league baseball together," Linda Hodgson remembers. "My husband Jim helped coach the boy's baseball teams with her husband. She was also a client of mine at the beauty shop, we had known her for years. Then later, when our boys were sophomores in high school my friend's son was headed down the wrong road, he was struggling with alcohol and drug abuse. She confided in me that she was having trouble with him, she didn't know what to do. I remember thinking that I needed to do something to help reach this boy, to help my friend, but I did not know how to help them."

Linda says that a few days later she went home one night and talked with her husband Jim and their sons, telling them about her friend's situation. That her friend's son, who they had known for years was in trouble, and the family needed their prayers.

On September 24, 1997, Linda's friend was tragically murdered by her son.

"After that happened God put it on my heart that I should do something to help troubled youth. I knew it was not my fault, that nothing I could have done would have prevented what happened to my friend. But still I felt this call on my life to help other young men like this young man and his family, but I had no idea what to do next."

It was about two or three weeks later, Linda was working in the beauty shop one day when another one of her clients, Susan Gilliland, came into the beauty shop to have her hair done. Susan proceeded to tell Linda that she wanted to go to the youth detention center in their hometown of Topeka, Kansas, and begin a Sunday school class for the young men in the detention center. Susan asked Linda if she would be interested in helping her begin that program and help her teach the Sunday school class.

"I specifically remember feeling goosebumps go up and down my arms. I knew immediately God was calling me to do this," said Linda.

It took about three weeks for Susan and Linda to be processed through the youth detention center's security clearance system. Once that process was completed, Susan and Linda began teaching Sunday school in the facility. Before long they had 30 to 40 teenagers in their Sunday school classes and 100 or so regularly attending weekly church services. In addition to teaching Sunday school, Linda also played the guitar and led the music for both services.

"I started in the prison ministry almost 25 years ago," recalled Linda. "I began initially teaching Sunday school. Then about 20 years ago, they decided to begin a Kairos Torch Ministry at the facility. We were excited because that was something they had not had before, and that would allow us to have one-on-one ministry relationships with the boys in the facility.

"The motto of Kairos Torch is love, love, listen, listen. I think one of the most important things we do is to listen to them, and you would think 'do teenagers really want to just sit and talk to old people?' and the answer is yes, they really do. Most of these young men have never had people who will sit across from them and spend time talking with them. I tell the young men today, that we have two sons, and that if I had been able to have an hour to sit across the table from them each week, that if we had spent more time together talking, we probably would have had a better relationship. It is this opportunity to mentor to these young men, the ability to talk with them, to develop relationships with them, and listen to all of things that are going on in their lives, that is a big part of what draws me and so many others to volunteer, to be a part of this ministry."

Kairos Torch had its beginnings in 1997 at a youth facility in Oklahoma. The Kairos Torch Ministry was developed to address the spiritual needs of young people ages 25 and younger who are incarcerated. The core of the Kairos Torch program is centered on one-to-one volunteer mentoring with the incarcerated youth.

The Kairos Torch program begins with a weekend retreat in the youth detention center or correctional facility. The ministry mission is to engage these young men they serve in an effort to bring some sense of balance into their lives. A Kairos Torch weekend offers a safe place for the youthful offenders, so that they may come to more clearly see their God-given potential, through the mentoring of mature, Christian volunteers.

The weekend program is centered around building trust and planting the seeds from which relationships may grow. There is a mask service that is held during this initial weekend, where the young men are encouraged to begin to break down the barriers created by the masques we all wear, as they begin to consider a new road, the new life offered to each of them through a relationship with Jesus Christ. This mask ceremony encourages them to strip away the masques they have hidden behind, and move them forward toward making better life choices while they are in the facility, and prepare them for a new life in Christ once they have served their time and are released.

Linda's husband, Jim, was a little concerned when Linda first began her prison ministry. As he said, these young men in the facility have committed serious crimes in their past. But as time passed Linda began to tell Jim about the young men she was meeting and her joy in helping them come to understand the Bible. Before long, Jim was visiting the facility with Linda when she taught Sunday school. It wasn't long after, that Jim became Linda's first volunteer recruit.

"Going to the Sunday school classes Linda and Susan were teaching and getting to know these young men has helped me to understand them a lot better," Jim said. "You know, there was a point in my life when I thought, when somebody messes up and they got put in prison, they deserved to be there, that's where they need to be, out of society. But now that I have worked with this ministry, I can see that these are just young men, they are no different than any other young man, they have just taken the wrong paths. You can look at them and say, 'I want to do my part to help them when they get out, to maybe plant the seed.' Then maybe later on when they do get released something that we talked about in our mentoring sessions might ring a bell with them, possibly make a difference in their lives even years later. We are there to plant seeds. That's what we are doing."

Over the years Linda has continued to recruit volunteers for the ministry. It was in 2005 that Linda reached out to another one of her beauty shop clients, and as only God could ordain it, unbeknownst to Linda at the time, this woman and her husband who also lived in Topeka, Kansas, would have a special connection to Ron Stiles.

"I invited them to be a part of the Kairos Ministry team because I knew they loved young people and that they would give it 100%." Linda continues, "I had been talking to Rhonda for four or five years about becoming a part of the ministry. Everyone is hesitant at first about going into a prison. Oftentimes it is something that people think they would not ever want to do."

Linda says that it was because of the way Rhonda and her husband loved people and were solid Christians that she continued to pursue them. "Eventually I convinced them to come to an informational meeting. They came to that meeting and decided that they were going to try it and see, and they have been onboard ever since."

"Linda was my hairdresser," Rhonda Han explained, "and she would say, 'I think you and Kevin would be so good at this and you would just love it.' And I would say we will think about it. Long story short we finally went to a meeting, and once you start with these kids, if you have any heart for it at all you are in."

Once Linda got Rhonda involved, she brought along her husband Kevin. The same Kevin Han who just so happened to be Ron Stiles' best friend, growing up together in Spring Hill, Kansas. At the time Kevin and Rhonda began working in the Kairos Torch Ministry, it had been over 40 years since Kevin and Ron Stiles had seen each other.

"I first met Ron when my family moved to Spring Hill when I was in the second grade, and we went to school together until my family moved to southeast Kansas when I was in the sixth grade. Ron was my best friend," Kevin said. "While I lived in Spring Hill, we played ball together and were in Cub Scouts together. Ron and I did all the things you do when you are kids with your best friend.

"We got into the Kairos Torch Ministry through Jim and Linda. I remember they were teaching Sunday school at that time, and they invited us to participate with them. We did everything we could initially to avoid it. But Linda was persistent. Eventually we went to an introductory meeting and became involved. We are now in our 15th year of ministry with Kairos Torch.

"The juvenile center where we minister is the only maximum-security juvenile facility in the state of Kansas. They are not messing around there. It is steel and concrete, and when the doors slam behind you it is noisy, it is definitely a prison. The boys volunteer to be a part of the Kairos program, they also have to be selected or approved by the officers, and the administration or the chaplain, so there is an approval process for them to be allowed to participate. The young men in our facility range in age from 12 to 22 ½ years old, and we have had the whole gamut of ages participating."

Kevin says that the young men in the facility have fairly limited visitation privileges with anyone from outside the prison. Kairos is one of those opportunities, so they look forward to it. They try and attract them with the food that is provided as part of the services. Their hope is that once the young men begin to come, they will hear something that speaks to them and they will continue to come to hear more of the Gospel message.

"One of the unique things about the Kairos Torch Ministry is that we have this three-day weekend that starts the mentoring process." Jim Hodgson continued, "We have been doing this long enough now that a lot of the young men who are in the prison know how this process works, and they know we have a lot of good food. There is no doubt that at first a lot of these young men come to the Kairos Weekend because they know that we have a lot of good food during this first weekend. But it is amazing to see how over the course of this first weekend the perception of the ministry and these young men's relationships with us change as we get to share Christ's teachings with them.

"It is remarkable to see the transformation in some of them. We cannot reach all of them, our role is to plant the seeds. Some of them will really begin to open up to us, and when that happens and they start communicating, we can see the difference the ministry is making in their lives. Some of these young men have really deep, painful family history's in their past. Most of them do not know their fathers, they don't have a father in their life. Sometimes their dad is in prison, sometimes their mom is in prison, sometimes brothers, sisters and cousins are in prison. Oftentimes they come from diverse and dark backgrounds, but when they take their masques off and they realize that they can relax and be themselves, you really see them begin to open up."

Linda says that the Saturday night meal is designed to be a pretty formal dinner. They have table cloths on the tables, everything matches and they bring in fresh flowers and they put them on all the tables. "I had this young man say to me recently that it had been five years since he had seen real flowers," says Linda. "We sit down together and we pass the food around family style. Many of these young men have never done that before, they don't know about passing food around a table. I have asked some of these young men before, 'Well how did you eat your food?' and they say they ate out of boxes or sacks. We try and give them a little taste of the lives most of us take for granted. It is very special to them and they appreciate it so much."

After the banquet on Saturday there is a Forgiveness Service that Jim regards as one of the highlights of the weekend.

"The Forgiveness Service that we have on Saturday night; it is a really special time. We have this rice paper that dissolves in water, and we have the young men write on this rice paper the names of the people in their lives who they want to forgive. Maybe it is themselves, maybe it is their mom or dad, or a brother or sister or someone else who has hurt them in their past, or someone they have committed a crime against, and they write these names on this rice paper. We also have paper masques there, and they write their feelings on these masques, to symbolize the masques that they feel that they wear. For instance, some may write 'anger' on the mask because they are angry. Then at the Saturday night Forgiveness Service we have what we call a God box, and we put all these masques in that box and then the box is destroyed. And they put the forgiveness items that were written on the rice paper in a bowl of water and watch it dissolve. It is a symbolic gesture of how Christ forgives our sins."

After the initial weekend the adult mentors meet together in pairs one-on-one with the young men on Thursday nights once a week for one hour. During these meetings the young men who are participating in the program learn to develop relationships with their volunteer mentors. Jim says that during these meetings the conversations can become pretty serious as the young men share their histories with their mentors.

"Sometimes we are successful reaching these young men and sometimes we are not," Rhonda Han explains. "That is just the way of it with many of these young men, many of whom are so troubled by what they have experienced, and as a result of these traumatic experiences some of them have then done some extraordinarily bad things. They are criminals, they are in prison because they have done bad things."

It was in the fall of 2009 while on a trip to Kansas City, Kevin and Rhonda decided to drive over to Spring Hill on the chance that they might catch up with Ron. This would have been over 40 years since Kevin had last seen Ron. Rhonda and Kevin went by Ron's parents' house, and soon Ron came over and the two old friends re-united. They exchanged contact information and then Kevin and Rhonda returned to Topeka. Then a few months later Ron reached out to Kevin and told him Nathan would be playing in a high school basketball game in Topeka and he invited Kevin to join him at Nathan's game. However, Kevin could not attend because he had a prior commitment with Kairos Torch.

"I didn't tell Ron at the time that I was going to be at a Kairos Torch meeting because it wasn't pertinent," Kevin says. "Then subsequent to that, the next thing that occurred was that I read in the paper about Nathan's death. That just struck an arrow through my heart, it affected me so deeply. So, I decided to write Ron a letter, in the letter I told him how sad I was to hear about Nathan, and I think in that letter too I also mentioned that we were doing prison ministry. By that time, he and Connie had begun the Nathan Project and he volunteered that if we were ever in need of Bibles for our ministry that he would be willing to supply them from the Nathan Project."

"When I called Kevin about meeting me at Nathan's basketball game in Topeka, he did not tell me his commitment that night was a meeting at the juvenile center with the youth there," Ron says. "Later after Nathan died, I received a beautiful letter from Kevin sharing his sympathy for our losing Nathan and telling me of the ministry work he and Rhonda were doing. From there we connected once again, the same bond we had as kids came back stronger than ever. Once again, God made the connection."

"It was a tremendous benefit to the Kairos Torch program when Ron and the Nathan Project began to supply our ministry with Bibles. Not only did we no longer have to buy Bibles, but these New Living Translation Study Bibles provided by the Nathan Project were written specifically for teens." Rhonda continues, "Having these study Bibles allowed the young men we are mentoring to be able to read the Bible with better understanding. That is a huge, huge advantage to the Kairos Ministry. In addition to that, the Nathan Project's affect has blossomed way beyond what Kairos does in the prison facility. We also distribute the Bibles in other ways throughout our community. We have one lady who is a volunteer in the ministry who regularly rides the bus, and when she meets people in need, she will ask people on the bus if they have a Bible, and if they don't, she will give them one. She also will leave the Bibles at bus stops like seeds for whoever will choose to take one, never knowing where the Bibles may be going or who they may help."

Linda says that it has been really interesting over the years to see how the young men they minister to relate to the Nathan Project Bibles, in large part because the ministry is dedicated to a young man their age, whose story is chronicled in the front and back covers of the Bible. A kid who played sports, whose goal was to bring his friends to Christ, and who wanted everyone to be able to have a Bible. For these young men, many of them who have never read the Bible before, it is helpful that the translation is written in today's English version because it is easier for them to understand. Linda has also seen a great benefit to the young men from the Bible footnotes and explanations strategically placed throughout the text, in making the scriptures more relevant to the situations these young men are experiencing in their lives, as they seek to know and understand what they are reading.

"Our son also helps distribute these Bibles," says Linda. "He is the director at the YMCA in Topeka. He gets the Bibles from the Nathan Project through Kevin and Rhonda, and gives them to kids who come in to play basketball and volleyball. In addition to that, he does a service once a month at the rescue mission here and he gives the Bibles away to people who come into the mission for assistance too. It's just amazing to see how many people get their hands on these Bibles. The Bibles have this bright orange and yellow cover, they are so noticeable; you can't mistake a Nathan Project Bible when you see one. You'll see someone with those orange and yellow Bibles and you can ask them, 'Well how did you get that Bible?', and they'll have some story of how they received it. It is pretty nice to hear all the various ways these Bibles are being distributed to people.

"We now are able to give a brand-new Nathan Project Bible to every young man who comes into our ministry. Actually, a lot of these kids we work with have never had their own Bible. In the prison facility, they are not allowed many personal items in their cells, but they are allowed to have a Bible. So, when they are given these Bibles, they are very important to them. They read them. Even the kids who you would definitely describe in the beginning as having been unchurched, they read their Nathan Project Bibles, and then every single week of our mentoring sessions we use that Bible."

Oftentimes on Thursday nights during their mentoring sessions the participants will read passages from the Bible and discuss these passages with their mentors. Jim says that once the young men are given the Nathan Project Bibles, they begin to read them in their cells when they are alone, and that over time you can see the differences in their lives as they begin to study the Bibles. Jim says that often the young men will come to their mentoring sessions and ask questions about what they are reading on their own, so the mentors know that these young men are reading and studying their Bibles.

"It's just a life-changing experience for these young men, to have these Bibles available for them to read," declares Jim. "Some of the young men will come the first week and say that they don't believe very much about the Bible, and their faith is pretty shallow; but once they receive the Bibles and begin to read them, you can see the change in them. Some of these guys, they are in prison for doing some pretty hardened things, and yet over time you begin to see them come around. You see the changes in their attitudes, and they come into our meetings and treat us with respect, something they probably didn't do on the outside."

Over the years once the Forgiveness Service has concluded and the mentoring sessions begin, there have been numerous instances where the young men participating in the Kairos Ministry have made the decision to follow Christ.

"We know that these decisions for Christ are being impacted by us being able to give these Nathan Project Bibles to the young men," insists Kevin. "We are lay people, so when one of the young people we are mentoring tells us they want to accept Christ into their lives, we ask the young man to then meet with clergy who are available to speak with them, and working with the clergy they give their lives to Christ. We are always thrilled when that happens. We don't always know about it at first; there are occasions when we hear about confessions for Christ that have happened in the facility with the chaplain after the fact, but we definitely see lives saved and lives changed as a result of the Kairos Ministry and the Nathan Project Bibles."

All of the mentors agree that having Nathan's story has been impactful to the young men in the Kairos program.

"We have been fortunate to have had Ron and Connie come into the facility and tell their story firsthand," Rhonda exclaims, "and you can see on the young men's faces the impact hearing that story has, how Nathan's story makes a personal connection with them. For them to see and hear the father of the young man who died and started the Nathan Project there with them telling the story firsthand, it has a huge impact on our young men when they have the opportunity to hear the story directly from the mother and father of Nathan.

"Whenever Ron speaks, they are excited to get a chance to meet the person who has provided the Bibles to them. It is a powerful message to see that someone cares enough about them to bring this story to them and give them a Bible. Whenever Ron speaks, once he finishes, there is a thunderous applause. They really love getting to meet Ron."

32

"It was about a month after Travis and I had been dating that Nathan Stiles passed away," Nicole said. "I remember that morning I was getting ready for school and my mom came in and told me Nathan had passed. It was at that point when I began realizing it does matter what I believe about God. That I needed to think more about going to church, and that even as a sixteen-year-old I needed to find out more about God. So, I went to his memorial service they had in the high school gym.

"Travis and I both knew Natalie and Nathan through school; they were always very kind. I was a very awkward middle schooler and not very social. Nathan was always really good at trying to include me, even when I was not good at trying to be included, and Natalie was always really kind. I wasn't best friends with either of them, but if I was in a project of any kind with them, they were always very kind and would never exclude anyone.

"The day Nathan died," Nicole recalled, "there was a feeling of heaviness in the school that day. You could have heard a pin drop. The reality that things like that can happen was very powerful. Even though we were only sixteen, to see that we are not guaranteed tomorrow, looking back on it now I can see that God was doing something in our school immediately after that happened. Then all these stories began to come out about Nathan, how Nathan had done this to serve someone, and he had done this to help someone, or just said a kind word to someone. Reflecting back, I know Nathan did that, during my interactions with him he was always positive and encouraging. The way he treated people affected so many lives.

"Nathan's parents and Natalie's response to Nathan's death showed me that there was something different about them. How even with Nathan's death they kept pointing people to God and to the Bible. Their example made me want to know more about faith. Up until that time I never really put together that the reason Nathan was such a great guy and that Natalie was so nice and easy to get along with was not about them, but it was about their relationship with God.

"It was just amazing to see how they were able to handle all of that, such a horrific situation, and get all those Bibles together in such short notice for Nathan's Celebration of Life Service. I didn't want to question where I would end up if something were to happen to me unexpectedly. I was pretty certain even at that point that Nathan was in heaven, and so I wanted to take God more seriously because I realized I was not guaranteed the next day. It was at Nathan's Celebration of Life Service when I chose to go down and get a Bible, my little brother got a Bible too.

"I went home that night and opened it up to Genesis chapter one. Later Travis texted me and asked 'if I was reading the Bible' and I said 'yes.' Then he asked 'where did I start' and I said 'Genesis' and he said 'why did you start there?' I said, 'don't you start at the beginning of a book?'"

Travis knew Nicole was having a hard time after Nathan died but as a sixteen-year-old himself he did not know how to help her. "When she got the Bible from the Celebration of Life Service that was a big help to her and going to the Nathan Project Bible studies helped her too."

Soon Nicole started going to church regularly. She went to church on Sundays with Travis, and the two of them went to a Nathan Project Bible study on Sunday night. Then she went to church with her mom on Saturday nights and youth group on Wednesdays with Travis.

"I started doing all the church things," Nicole remembers. "I had a close friend who went to the same church and youth group as Travis so that was nice that I had a friend there.

"After Nathan died, we went to a Nathan Project Bible study, led by one of our youth group leaders. We were reading through Luke. Reading through the book of Luke you get to know who Christ is and see His ministry. I really appreciated how our youth pastor cared about us and how he invested in me. He was really good at teaching. He and our other youth leaders, they just loved me really well. That was something I could really tell was different about them. From that experience I began to see that the people who loved God really loved other people well. When I first started showing up to youth group, Sunday school and Bible study they didn't just treat me as though I was Travis' girlfriend, they treated me as though they really wanted to get to know me and support me, that I had value.

"I really appreciated the Bible studies and the way they were taught because it gave me another place to learn. I am really thankful for that foundation of getting into the Word and seeing who Christ is and how they taught me."

Even though Nicole was attending church services and Bible studies she had not chosen to follow Christ yet. At that point she described herself as, "questioning and seeking but I still hadn't committed my life to Christ." During this seeking out period there were times when Nicole would see Travis and her friends and they would be so confident in their faith that Nicole would think, "'I am doing all the right things, and I am reading my Bible but at that point I did not have the confidence in my faith they had. That continued for a few months until February of the next year. One Sunday the pastor at our church was talking about how personal prayer is; about how God cares about us, and that He will never abandon us. That He loves us unconditionally, and it just clicked for me. I don't think before that day I had fully realized that. That was the day I chose to really follow Christ."

It was their junior year in high school when Nicole chose to follow Christ and become a Christian. Looking back on it now Nicole recalls a time when she and Travis had just started dating and Travis asked Nicole if she was a Christian. "I said 'Yes, I am, what else would I be?', and I was thinking 'I really hope his family doesn't read their Bible everyday like crazy Christians,' and now I am one of them!"

During their senior year Nicole told Travis that once they graduated, she would like to go to college at Fort Hays State University in Hays, Kansas and Travis said his brother went to college there. "God really opened a lot of doors to make it possible for me to go to Fort Hays," Nicole said.

"That summer before I was about to go off to college," Travis recalls, "I still did not know how to live my life, but I remember praying for two things. One was that God would give me a job while I was in school so I could earn my own money while I was there, and two, that he would put me in a place where I could grow in my faith. The summer before I was to start college we went out to Hays to get registered and when we went to the bookstore to get my books for school the lady who was helping me asked if I could move some books for her, then as soon as I did she asked me, 'Do you want a job?' and just like that God met my first need. So that first day when I came back to start classes, I had a job without ever having to go to an interview, and that confirmed to me it was a clear answer to prayer.

"My other prayer was that God would give me a place where I could grow in my faith. The first day after my parents left, I came across this place called Christian Challenge, and they invited me in, and wanted me to be a part of their group. Christian Challenge was a place of solid biblical teaching. Being a part of that group helped me live my faith while I was in college."

"Our freshmen year we went to vision groups with Christian Challenge, which were Bible study groups," Nicole recalls, "and the first time we were there, they said that if

150

anyone needs a Bible we have one that you can borrow, and these people were going up and taking them to use, but many of these Bibles were old and worn, and they could only be borrowed for an evening at a time before being returned."

It was at that meeting when Nicole remembered a conversation her mother had with Ron Stiles the summer before Nicole left to go off to college.

"Ron had seen my mom somewhere and he told her that 'if Nicole ever has a need for Bibles out in Hays, Kansas let me know.' So, I texted Christian Challenge and let them know that I was new to the program and they really did not know me well at that point, but I knew of a way they could get Bibles for free that could be given away in their ministry if they wanted them. They responded, 'yes, they would like to have them.' This was probably the first week of school. By Labor Day weekend we took back 50 or 100 Bibles to school with us. Then these people who did not have a Bible were able to get one and keep it. It was also really cool to me to know that I was a part of that, that I had gotten my first Bible from the Nathan Project, and then I was able to be a part of giving Bibles to others who did not have one.

"A couple of years later we ran out of Bibles again, so we requested some more Bibles from Ron and again he supplied us free Bibles. Since then every couple of years we have gotten free study Bibles from the Nathan Project. To date Christian Challenge has been gifted around 350 Bibles for our campus ministry from the Nathan Project. We have them set out on our tables at our large group meetings and we give them to our student leaders to take with them as they share the Gospel. If people we minister with don't have a Bible, we are able to give one to them.

"It has been really cool, over the years to go around campus and see people with those orange Nathan Project Bibles. Sometimes I go up to them and say, 'Hey, have you read the story in the front and back covers of the Bible? In the story it talks about how the Nathan Project began and how the first night they gave away several hundred of those Bibles, and I was one of those people who got one and that is part of my faith journey.'

"It has been great to be able to share with people how God has been working in my life and how God has allowed me to share those Bibles with so many students over the years. I know several students who have gotten those New Living Translation Bibles who tell me how they have been encouraged by how easy it is to read them because they were written in today's English. I know that was an issue for me as a new Christian trying to read and understand the King James version. The King James versions can be difficult to understand. By being able to read and understand what the Bible is saying they are able to see that it is relevant to us today."

Nicole and Travis agreed that becoming a part of campus ministry when they went to school gave them a place where they could plug into with people who had similar values. Being involved in campus ministry gave them the accountability they needed during that crucial transition time in their lives. It is easy for college students to get caught up in the temptation of partying, drinking, or any of the other things that college life throws at students on campus. Without the community of college ministry, it would be easy for freshmen especially, to withdraw from others and seek to get their identity from school work, the pursuit of shallow success or comfort.

Another surprising thing to Nicole and Travis were the number of new believers in the group, that there were so many new believers who did not know Christ before going to college.

It was her participation in campus ministry that led Nicole down an unexpected career path.

"I felt really loved by the people at Christian Challenge and how the people there were pursuing God and wanting to share that with others. So, I wanted to join the leadership team. Not because I felt like I had anything to offer, but because I wanted to be a part of what they were doing. My sophomore year I was a chemistry major, but during that year God started to show me that was not what He wanted for me.

"The only thing I knew was that I wanted my job to be sharing my faith with people, but I had no idea how that could happen because I knew I needed to make a living when I graduated.

"Later, Travis was on a mission trip in Kenya for seven weeks between our sophomore and junior years. It was during that time when our director met with me and asked if I would pray about joining the campus ministry staff. I prayed about it for a couple of weeks and it became pretty clear that was something God had been preparing me for and gifting me to do. So, I changed my major to general studies because I did not want to have a backup plan. I joined the staff in August of 2015.

"It is really cool working in campus ministry with college students. College students are at this pivotal point in their lives where they are open to a lot of new things, trying to figure out what they believe. Whether they come from a church background or not, no matter what their faith background, they are trying to figure out what they believe when they come onto a college campus. You have four years with the students, and during those years they are making choices like, 'What am I going to do for a year? Who am I going to marry? What am I going to believe and where am I going to live?' They are open to so many things, the flexibility and the adaptability that they have. You are able to challenge them very easily because they have the capacity for it and they have the free time to spend in the word. They also have the desire to grow and they have the ability to do so. They have these four years and during that time they have this training ground to get a degree, but also to develop their careers for the rest of their lives, and to really build their faith upon that."

Travis and Nicole say it is really cool to see the freshmen come in and be nervous about their faith, and then to see them grow in their faith over four years. "There were a couple of students," Nicole says, "who came in as freshmen four years ago that I was able to pour myself into. They graduated last year. It was really sad to see them go, but it is also exciting to see them go out on their own."

"It is different sitting across from a high school student and asking them if they know God and talking with an adult college student," Travis claims. "It is a really unique place to do ministry. It is a cool position to be in to see college students grow and become mature in their faith. Our job is to ask those questions and to walk with them as they figure out what they believe, and what a blessing to see that happen. There are three guys who just graduated, seeing the fruit of investing in them and showing them what the kingdom of God is like, and then seeing them actually choosing to do that with their free time. It is a really rich blessing to be a part of that."

"Our culture really does not see the importance of God's Word," Nicole expressed. "Helping them see that God's Word is relevant, that it is true, and the standard by which we need to live. God's Word is what we can sift everything else the world is shouting at us through. Helping students see the importance of God's Word is one of the biggest goals I have with the girls I meet with on a regular basis. My goal is to have the girls that I meet with know that God's Word is important and it is relevant, and that they need to be regularly reading their Bible to know what God says, because if you don't know what the truth is, how are you going to measure anything else?"

Nicole graduated in December of 2015. Travis graduated the following May. They were married in March 2016. Since graduating college, they have both been a part of the campus ministry team at Fort Hays with Christian Challenge.

One of the challenges Travis and Nicole are seeing Christian students dealing with as they come to college is trying to prepare for life in a secular world while maintaining God's role in their lives. Students have the expectation that once they get out of school, they need to have a job, which is good, and that they are there to learn a certain thing so they can get a job. At the same time these young people are also learning that their true identity comes from their relationship with Jesus. The reality is that as Christians, their place in God's Kingdom is what's most important. They say many times they see students who come to campus who are Christians and they have this mentality that God fits into their life, and fits into their job. That's a huge issue that they try to work through with students. In their ministry work they have the opportunity to show students that the reality is that their job, and their family, and their career, and all of those relationships are meant to fit into God's Kingdom and into His will. They say that is a complete 180 degree turn from what the American Dream teaches us. That is a huge barrier that many students have when it comes to knowing God better, that they are there to glorify God and love Him well, instead of God loving them well and just fitting into their lives. It re-orders their priorities.

Both Nicole and Travis agree that one of the best parts of their ministry work is seeing how people grow in their faith by reading God's Word regularly. When these students read their Bible, it changes them and they can see the difference: their attitudes are better, their quiet time with God improves, they have more peace. They say it has been rewarding to see how these students realize the importance of reading God's Word regularly and how some of them have re-oriented their lives, some of whom have gone through really difficult things. Some of their students have told them how they can see a difference in themselves when they are getting into God's Word regularly versus when they are not, the peace versus the anxiety they experience. "I have seen that is true with many of the students we disciple," Travis said. "God's Word is good. It is truth that you can measure everything else by. We tell students, not to just take our word for the power of God's Word, but to get into it for themselves, so they can see the blessings of reading God's Word. Some of the students we have discipled, are now discipling other students with God's truth.

"Like showing them, through reading the Psalms, that it is okay to share with God how you are feeling when you pray or when you are upset. It has been awesome to see the students grow as they learn how to approach God through prayer. To see them have a better picture and understanding of who God is and who they are in Him, giving them more confidence and freedom through Christ has been cool.

"We had this one student who came to college with a strong sports background, having been really good at high school sports." Travis continues, "When he got to college that didn't matter to anyone. He had been a star at his high school, but now his identity had been really shaken. His identity was in sports and now it was gone, so where do you turn? Showing him what to do with that now, that you take God's Word, and begin to show it to him, so that he can begin to see the principles that God tells us, whether it is God's promises or how to live helpfully. Over time, he began to see that his identity in Christ was unchangeable, and that had more value than anything you could place your identity in, outside your relationship with Christ. Now he memorizes scripture, and he really values that, because God's Word is in his heart now. That is something that he thinks about constantly. Reading God's Word, and his faith in Christ, has changed his perspective and made him a much more relaxed person, as well as more peaceful and assured.

"There was another student who had an issue with sarcasm. It was something he had grown up around in his family in the way they talked to each other. I began to see how sarcasm tears down people. It doesn't build them up the way the Bible tells us to. God teaches us to build people up all the time, when sarcasm is the opposite of that, it puts us down. So, I showed him that and told him he knew it was wrong, but he did not know how to fix it. I told him God tells us so many times in the Bible that we are supposed to be encouraging. Being an encourager makes us more effective leaders and it also builds up the church. It has helped him understand how to be an encourager and someone who blesses other people, instead of using words to harm. Now he has seen how God's Word affected his life and others.

"God's Word when you apply it to people's lives, it changes them and shows them that God loves them."

33

As the Kansas City Youth for Christ video, *Jose's Story*, begins, you hear a young man's voice saying;

"He told this one recruit, 'Hey Man, you're not going to make it in the hood until you make it on the news. When you make it on the news is when you are going to make it in this life, alright.'

"I didn't grow up deprived or nothing. My mom loved me and stuff like that. I was bored. Life was dull to me. I was told as a kid one time, 'If you are going to sell drugs, you better do it right. Don't sell nothing under a hundred dollars because that ain't worth going to jail for.'

"Growing up I took that as my motto. Thirteen or fourteen is when I got into that lifestyle real deep. I fought for anything and everything. All my homeboys and friends in my neighborhood, they had my number, knowing that if they called me, I would pull up, and depending on what the situation was, me and a couple of my homeboys we would take care of whatever was going on.

"I built up so much money and credibility in my neighborhood that I took over my own block. It gave me a lot of credibility with the gang I was in. I wanted to hurt people. I didn't care who it was or what gang they were in, I was ready.

"But you only get away with so much, until it all comes back to you." ·

* * *

Randy Herold accepted Christ in 1975. Shortly thereafter Randy felt that God was calling him to begin holding Bible studies for youth in his home. In 1995, Randy attended a church revival meeting in Florida, after attending this meeting he became involved in a small group ministry seeking to reach youth. The first night they had nineteen kids meeting in his home.

Later in 1997, Randy went to lunch with the Florida Region's Youth for Christ Director who knew of Randy's passion to minister to young people. That day the director asked Randy if he would consider working with Youth for Christ. Randy joined Youth for Christ and continued working as a part of that ministry for the next 22 years. He moved to Kansas City with Youth for Christ in the winter of 2009 to spend more time with his daughter and grandchildren who lived in the area.

When Randy moved to Kansas City, Youth for Christ did not have a ministry counseling program in the juvenile detention centers in the Kansas City metropolitan area. So, they asked Randy to begin working with law enforcement to arrange for Youth for Christ personnel to start a counseling program for kids in the detention centers in the Kansas City area. At first Randy did not want to work in prison ministry. But after considering the importance of the work he chose to do it. It took him about 5 ½ months to get that program started. Randy began counseling in the detention center in March of 2010. He met Jose Vega about three months later.

Jose says that he would describe his life before he met Randy as someone who found themself stranded on an island that was going under water, with little hope of rescue. Before Jose was arrested, he says he had plenty of opportunities to change his lifestyle, but he passed on those options. "I was like the man that God sent people to help him on that sinking island, two in boats and one in a helicopter to save him, and the drowning man sends those people away. Then later the man drowns and goes to heaven and he asks God, 'Why didn't you save me?' and God says, 'I sent two boats and a helicopter.'

Before he went to jail, Jose says there were plenty of moments, opportunities, when God sent people into his life to help him, but at the time, he didn't recognize that God was working in his life.

These moments he refers to now as the waves, that God sends to turn us away from the roads that often lead us down the path to pain and heartache. "Some waves lap at your toes, and some of us ignore these waves," Jose says. "Then, there are other waves that sweep you over and knock you to the ground. For some of us, we don't respond to the small gentle waves. It takes the larger waves that smack us in the face, those waves that knock us down to get our attention.

"There were moments in my life, when God sent people to help me. Looking back on it now, I can see that God was sending me small waves to get my attention, and help me see that He was reaching out, trying to help me. Some of us, we can't see the small waves God is sending to reach us, to save us.

"In my life, it took the jail door shutting behind me to get my attention," said Jose.

"I could have stopped before, like when my friend passed away. But I missed those chances to turn my life around because at that time I was too confident, too cocky, too into myself, and too focused on the world around me. I was focused only on how this world is, and how I wanted to see myself in this world. I wanted to get my persona out there, so I missed all of those opportunities."

Jose's grandfather is a believer, and Jose remembers him talking to Jose, mentioning scripture verses to him when he was a kid growing up. His grandfather would spend time with Jose and try to reach him with those verses, but at the time

Jose was resistant, he says he missed those waves of opportunity too.

"Those were moments that could have taken me somewhere else, but I missed those chances," admits Jose.

Every night we turn on the news or pick up the evening newspaper and we see stories of young people living among us who are dealing with circumstances more difficult than most of us will ever be able to fully comprehend. Oftentimes we may get a glimpse of another person's life from a distance, and we can be quick to judge the choices they have made or their lifestyle. Because from our perspective, we cannot understand what it is like to walk in that person's shoes.

For most of us, we can't begin to understand what it is like to grow up in the circumstances many of our young people are facing today. We will never see first-hand the compromised places they are living, the neighborhoods that limit their choices, the dangerous situations they find themselves in, in most cases beyond their control. For us to truly understand as Christians how to reach people who find they are traveling down one of those dead-end roads in life, it is critical that we begin to see what their lives are like from their perspective.

Randy says that after working with youth for over 25 years, his experience has taught him that people who are wanting to work in ministry with young people who have been exposed to gangs, drugs and all the violence they see on a daily basis, we need to understand where they are coming from and what their lives have been like. We should not judge them only by what they have done, because in most cases, their choices were very limited.

"There will be times when working with troubled youth when these kids will not do what they have promised; they will not show up at first until they see that they can trust you. Often in the beginning, young people will commit to doing things and then change their minds.

"One of the realities we have to remember when we think about the lifestyle many of our at-risk young people are living today," Randy continues, "is that many of these young people don't look at life past 24 hours. They are thinking, 'what can I do right now?'"

According to Randy, most of the troubled youth he is counseling today, when he first engages them, he finds their emotional lives are so scarred by what they have experienced that they don't think about the future. Randy regularly works with teenagers who have come from environments that are so dangerous and bleak, where they are living with the violence of the drug culture all around them, that they do not believe or even hope that they will live past the age of 21.

"When I first got into the gang lifestyle it was the drugs that attracted me," Jose said. "It was the money, you were a part of a group, no one could touch us or say anything to us. The guys who were in the gangs, from the outside it looked like they were having the time of their lives. It wasn't about going out and shooting at people. It was about the macho attitude that came with being a part of a gang. We're this gang, we control this area."

Jose and the kids in his neighborhood grew up seeing the gang life all around them, and not just the gang life, but drugs and violence also. Jose says he first started smoking pot when he was under the age of ten. He started smoking pot because it was available all around him. People he knew growing up were in cartels, gangs, and gang bangers. "There were gangsters all around us when I was a kid. I don't know how to explain it any better than that," Jose said.

He began selling drugs when he was around 12 years old. The only reason he said he didn't start selling before then was because he couldn't get it. He sold marijuana at first, a little bit here, and a little bit there.

The first time Jose saw someone gunned down; he was 13 years old. He remembers that he was so into the gang lifestyle at the time, that seeing someone die didn't affect him much. In Jose's mind, "It was like they should have known this comes with being in a gang, it is part of the street life, so they should have known this was going to happen to them."

Then a few years later, there was an event that hit Jose hard and washed over him like a tidal wave, knocking him tumbling to the ground. This event set into motion a series of moments that would change Jose's life.

"When my best friend died before I went to the detention center, it was like 'screw it, everyone is dead.' And I'm not going to let people kill my friends again. My friend died two weeks before the fourth of July, and I got arrested shortly after that. It was after being arrested that Randy and I met; I was 17 then. Going to jail was good for me, because I had to slow down. Before going to jail and meeting Randy, I was on a full speed run to nowhere. At that point in my life, I was a bad kid, I was going down the path to nowhere, and I didn't care. I was angry and depressed; I was upset about my friend dying."

Randy remembers the first day they met, Jose was so emotional when he was telling Randy about his friend dying, that Jose could hardly talk.

"I was so broken up at that time," Jose claimed. "I was mad at everybody. I didn't want to listen to nobody."

It was then that Randy began to work with Jose, mentoring him and counseling him. Soon, on one of their visits, Randy presented Jose with a Nathan Project Study Bible. Later, after some time talking and reading the Bible together, Jose gave his life to Christ, and the transformation in Jose's life began.

What was so amazing to Randy about Jose, was that when Jose picked the Nathan Project Bible up and started to read it, he could interpret the Bible like somebody who had been in college. "That is what amazed me about it, because in the beginning when he first began to read it, Jose had absolutely no understanding of the Bible. He knew a few things from going to church as a kid, but it was like he picked up that Bible and the Lord started showing things to him."

"When I started reading the Bible, it was like everything that I was reading started hitting me so hard," Jose exclaimed, "reading some of those passages, I felt like Paul when the scales fell off of his eyes. For the first time in my life, I started seeing things clearly.

"I have been working with Randy for five years now. Before I met Randy, I was not doing the best things. I was out with my friends trying to find excitement. We were staying out late and gang banging. We did a lot of stupid things that I look back on now and say, 'was that really me? Did I really do that?'

"When I went to prison, I was in a really bad spot at that time. I had just lost a really good friend of mine. He passed away two weeks before, and at the time I'm not going to lie, I was seeing red. Everything was like in a shade of red, and I didn't really care too much about people, life was depressing. When I first got into juvenile detention I got into a fight. Just because I was upset, and I didn't want anyone telling me what I could and couldn't do.

"Randy spent time talking with me. Randy was an anchor for me, we need those people who are anchors in our lives. So many people were being brought into my life that could have helped me before I went to jail. But if you are not slowing down, you can't capture those moments. It took jail slowing me down to meet a person like Randy, who came in like a boat or a helicopter to take me off of that sinking island. I believe it was all part of God's plan in a way.

"And the Nathan Project Bible that Randy gave me was really impactful. I read my Bible and I prayed a lot while I was in the detention center. I read in the Bible how it is important to walk around with a prayerful mind. So, I try to do that. I am walking around now praying to God all day.

"I feel like meeting Randy has opened a big door for me. I needed someone to open a door for me and Randy was that guy. I see now that everyone's life is full of ups and downs; my life is in a much better place now than where I was before I met Randy.

"Randy didn't save my life, because it was God who saved my life, but he was the one who helped me get my life back on track. Now I always try and go to anything Randy asks me to do with a group or another kid that he is ministering to, so that one day I might be a Randy to them, that I might be able to build that bond with them, to open that door for them."

Jose says that the text in the New Living Translation Bibles given away by the Nathan Project was different than any other Bible he and the other kids in the detention center had seen before. The bright orange and yellow cover design of the Nathan Project Bible according to Jose was eye catching, and the footnotes in the margins and the sides of the Bible were quick to catch his attention. He found the sections in the bottom of the Bible that relates what you are reading to today's times, and the stories of the people who share their personal testimonies, made him more curious about what the Bible scriptures were saying. The footnotes that explain the key points of the Bible stories piqued his interest and made him want to read more.

"A lot of the people who were getting the Nathan Project Bibles who were in the facility with me at that time, they were also young, and they didn't have much of a Christian background. So, in the past when they would have picked up another Bible and tried to read it, it was like question, after question, after question, and they didn't understand what they were reading. Reading the Nathan Project Bible made us think, it got us wondering; how would I interpret what I am reading in my life?"

Jose says that when juveniles are in jail, sitting in their cells, they have no one to talk to, most of the time they are alone in their cells. That was the time many of the juveniles would read their Bibles.

"When I was reading through the New Living Translation Nathan Bible," Jose said, "it was the 'I wonder' sections that are found in the Bibles that really helped me to understand and apply what I was reading, because it answered the questions that I would have about the passages and what they meant after I had read the verses."

"I don't remember when I first saw the Nathan Project Bibles," Randy said, "or when I first met Ron even, but what I do remember is that once we got the Nathan Project Bibles, so many kids would pick those Bibles up and take them and read them that would not have read the other Bible versions, because they could not understand them.

"Another thing I have noticed with the Nathan Bibles," Randy continued, "is that the juveniles would take the Bibles and thumb through them, and they would find the notes that explain the key points of the passages or the characteristics of the personality profiles of the Bible characters, and they would stop and read those, and that got them more interested in reading the scriptures.

"I would say that of these kids that are reading the Nathan Project Bibles, the number one part they are using is the glossary. They go to the back of the Bibles and they look up the topics that are meaningful to them."

Randy says that numerous kids in the detention centers would tell him when something happened to them, maybe they would get mad or upset with someone, they would go back in their cells and take the Nathan Project Bibles, and go to the glossary section and find the emotional topic they were experiencing, and go read about that term. For instance, they would look up the term angry, or depression, and they would go to the glossary and search out all the verses that related to those topics and read them. They may not have read the whole chapters, but they would look up those specific verses based upon the topic they were trying to figure out. That is what Randy says impressed him the most about the Nathan Bibles.

"It was amazing to see the positive impact the Nathan Project Bible was having on these kids. What I mean by amazing, is that 9 out of 10 of those kids had absolutely no prior Biblical understanding. That is why I think the Nathan Project Bible works so well with kids, because it explains the verses and the way the Bible is written with the footnotes the kids can understand what they are reading."

Soon after Jose began to earnestly read his Bible, he began his own Bible study with the other inmates.

"Once Jose began leading the Bible studies, we would meet around the table with several of the other kids in the detention center. Jose started telling everybody the answers to their questions by reading and studying his Bible on his own, and from there our Bible studies just kind of exploded." Randy says, "When Jose left the juvenile detention center, he had two years to serve and he went to prison in Topeka, Kansas. What I found out later through other kids, is that Jose started a Bible study in Topeka also, and held that Bible study on his own for a year with different kids in that facility too."

"I started helping kids when they had questions," Jose declared, "and those Nathan Project Bibles, they gave away so many of those Bibles in the facility in Topeka too."

It was there in Topeka, that Jose became a part of the Kairos Torch Ministry program. In Topeka, Jose met Jim and Linda Hodgson and Kevin and Rhonda Han. The same Kevin Han who was Ron Stiles' boyhood friend from Spring Hill over 40 years earlier.

"The thing about jail, is that a lot of times when things don't go so smoothly, we would be locked down or we couldn't leave the pod. In those times, I would go back to my cell and sit down and read my Bible. Whatever touched me as I read, I would write it down, and we would talk about it the next day in our pods, and the Bible studies started like that. I wouldn't try to push religion or God on anyone. I would wait for them to open up to me. I feel like I have a better connection with people, when I let them open up to me and they ask me questions about God.

"I feel my best teaching is one-on-one or in small groups now. What I try to do, what makes me feel better about my life in my heart, is I try to plant seeds into people's lives. I know that not everyone is going to be saved, but what I take joy in, is that I can try and help them. If that seed grows in them by the grace of God then that is going to be great. I don't like to push too hard on people to believe."

Sometimes Jose says he finds that the people he is ministering to get discouraged when things in their lives are not going their way. As new believers they can soon begin to lose faith, when they are facing trials, they can begin to doubt God is real.

Jose tells the people he ministers to today, many of who are new Christians trying to read the Bible for the first time, to slow down, take a breath and read something, and if you don't understand something you are reading ask questions. He has found that when people first begin to read their Bibles and they don't understand what they are reading immediately, they should not feel bad because they don't understand, they don't understand because they are new Christians and God is just beginning to show these things to them.

"It is like what we learn by studying the Ten Commandments found in the Bible," Jose continues, "those commandments in the Bible are there to show us that we can't live a life without Christ. We have to live our life every day dependent on Christ's grace alone or we're not going to meet Christ. We can't live a life of faith without Him, and these commandments show us that.

"Most people don't understand that there are trials and tribulations so that there is belief," Jose says. "One girl asked me, 'What's a blessing?' I said a blessing is after I have succeeded in going through God's trial, God gave me a blessing. It's not that God gave me a blessing because I was a good person. No, it's that I fought through a trial that God put in front of me."

Looking back on it now Jose is convinced that a trial even as large as him going to prison, was not a bad thing for him. "That whole jail experience for me was not a bad point in my life. I have had way worse experiences in my life than being in jail. I see now that being in jail was a part of God's plan for me. I know now that God has a bigger plan for me."

Randy says that throughout his mentoring career, he has met numerous people who are believers today, who tell him that if they had not gone to prison, they would not have found the Lord. For them it was the best place they could have been, going to prison was a reality check. Jose is one of those people.

"Now when I get down and discouraged and when I talk to God about situations in my life, I pray, I ask God to take over," Jose exclaimed. "Because I know that I don't have the strength to do it on my own. As a person, as a human being my strength is limited. I have a limited amount of strength, I have a limited amount of tolerance, and on my own I can't do it. But when I am facing a trial today, I say 'God, if you think this trial that I am facing is going to lead me in the right way and be good for me, then take full advantage of it.' I just take whatever happens after that. If something bad happens I take it as a lesson learned, because if things don't turn out the way I wanted them to I know it's not the way God wanted it, so I don't beat myself up over those things anymore.

"God's got such a big plan for all of us, we can't grasp the heavens and what the heavens can show us. Sometimes we need a set back; we need those moments to clear our minds. I believe every day that I walk with Christ. I am praying now 24/7, and I am thankful for the little things in life, and I say 'thank you Lord,' because I appreciate those things. God and I walk together with a strong bond.

"Reading the Bible and accepting Christ changed me in the way I thought about life. It changed the way I felt about life itself. Before Christ, I didn't think life was that big a deal. Once I saw that God accepted me, and now that I have prayed and accepted Christ as Lord, I am seeing a different life.

"I could not see at that time what God had planned. As people we oftentimes see pictures too small. Now that I have been saved, I see things different. It's like Jesus told His disciples, you are still seeing things as humans, you are still seeing things as this world. We don't understand this new body that we are going to get, this new life that we are going to have. We often lose sight of what accepting Christ really means to us. We can't fully understand it now because we are human. We see things from an earthly perspective.

"That's how I believe life is, we have got our own decisions to make left or right, but God sees what our lives are going to become, God sees what's at the end of that street. God knows that if you keep driving downtown like you have lost your mind and you keep hitting these one-ways then you are going to hit another car and you're going to die. I think that's where I was before Christ. I was living that life. I was out there shooting at people, out there selling drugs every day. That was me driving down one-way streets the wrong way. That was a picture of my life then, before I met Christ, when I kept hitting dead-end roads, and finding myself in those places that God does not want us to be.

"But for all of us, once we accept the Lord, no matter what our life was like before, we are new creatures in Christ. Look at Moses' life. Moses was not perfect, Moses was a murderer, and yet God used him. Why can't we have that kind of a relationship with God? Even if we have a past, God can still use us."

* * *

Randy remembers another kid who benefited greatly from receiving the Nathan Bible. When he got out of jail, he wanted Randy to come to his house and lead a Bible study. Jose came along with Randy and they started a Bible study there. Randy says, "to give you a little background on the type of trials this young man had endured, this young person asked me, 'How do you love somebody who set you up and got you shot and your best friend killed?' This young man's life was changed too by having a Nathan Project Bible."

Randy now sends Jose and this young man and some of the other young people he mentors, Bible verses every day on his phone, and every day these young people send Randy back notes about the Bible verses. "All of these kids have been impacted by praying to accept the Lord, and having a Nathan Bible played a large role in their salvations, because they all used it," declares Randy.

When asked about how Randy's intervention and receiving the Nathan Project Bible and hearing Nathan's story impacted him, Jose had this to say:

"The thing that happened to Nathan caused great sadness, but God figured out how to make something great out of even this tragedy. God sometimes takes bad things and makes a great impact for good, like with these Bibles. If I had never gone to jail, I would have never met Randy and received a Bible. I am just one of the people who have read these Nathan Project Bibles and had a really great experience from having it. Not everyone is going to be able to pick up the older versions of the Bible and read them, because they can't understand what they are reading.

"When I was in the detention center and we first learned about Nathan's story, we watched a video about Nathan and the Nathan Project. It was interesting hearing his story. In my mind I could see where God probably had something huge planned for that guy, and then there was the devastation of what happened to Nathan. But what has come from his family giving away the Bibles, it was as if God said we are going to take this tragedy and make something so big come from it. I would have never known about Nathan and his family if it wasn't for Nathan's story and his family's drive to be out there sharing his love for God by giving away these Bibles."

34

April 18, 1996, in an open field just outside of Lincoln, Nebraska, a small private plane piloted by University of Nebraska football player Brook Berringer crashed shortly after takeoff, killing both Brook and his girlfriend's brother, Tobey Lake, in the accident. A few days later their funeral was held at the Max Jones Fieldhouse in their hometown of Goodland, Kansas.

Sitting in the fieldhouse that day, also from Goodland, was high school senior Michele Hallagin. Michele, like Brook, was an accomplished athlete. She was the Kansas 4-A Volleyball Player of the Year her junior and senior years of high school. Michele would go on to attend Wichita State University on a full athletic volleyball scholarship where she would be recognized as First Team Academic All-American her senior year.

"I was sitting with our show choir from school in The Max that day, we sang a song or two for the funeral. Brook was a hometown hero in our small town of about 5,000. He played quarterback for Nebraska and contributed to their two national championships in '94 and '95. As the memorial service was nearing its start time, we got word the Nebraska football team was running late from Lincoln so we waited for them to come before it started. When they finally arrived, seeing all of them walk in together through the tunnel of The Max still gives me goosebumps. It was eerily quiet in a gym that's normally roaring with excitement."

While sitting among the crowd of over 4,000 that day Michele says she heard many inspiring stories from the people who took the stage to speak about Brook. And as she was listening to the speakers share their memories of Brook, she began to clearly see the important role faith had played in Brook's life and she began to consider faith in Christ in a new way. During Brook's service she felt God speak to her, tugging at her heart.

Michele remembers that she was in awe and humbled as she listened to the different speakers including Tom Osborne, Ron Brown, and Art Lindsay speak about Brook's life, his character, and his relationship with Christ.

"I heard so many ironic things that happened with Brook's death that it convinced me there was something bigger in this life."

Like in many small towns, Michele's family and the Berringers knew each other. Rollie Hallagin, Michele's dad, was a high school football referee and he and her mom Jean knew Brook as not only a great football player, but also a great 'kid.' Michele still remembers, "When Brook graduated high school, we went to his graduation reception at his house. I took a piece of paper with me and had him sign it. When our family watched the '94 Nebraska national championship game, we sat that paper by the TV."

While speaking at Brook's funeral Nebraska coach Tom Osborne said Brook had more character than any other football player he had ever coached, and he had coached a lot of players, around 2,000 he said. Hearing this, Michele thought, "how could a guy like this have died? Why?"

Art Lindsay was Brook's prayer partner. Michele recalls hearing at the memorial service, "Art said he had recently asked Brook what he wanted to see happen over the next four to five years. Despite Art thinking of the temporal (like Brook playing in the NFL), Brook was thinking about the eternal as he replied, 'he simply wanted to grow in his relationship with Jesus Christ because it was the greatest thing that had ever happened to him.' He said Brook was currently reading the devotional, *My Utmost for His Highest* by Oswald Chambers. Art said Brook liked to do his devotional each morning. The devotional for April 18th, the day Brook died, was "Be ready for sudden surprise visits from God." Brook would have read this before going out that day. Brook was ready. He was prepared.

"Art went on to say that Brook was expected to go in the NFL draft the upcoming weekend. He said, 'Brook was still drafted, he was drafted #1 overall, drafted by God. That was the best draft he could hope for.'" Michele thought, "More than the NFL draft? There must be something bigger than this life!"

The Max Jones Fieldhouse is a premier facility in the Tri-State region of Kansas, Colorado and Nebraska. It was built in the 1960s and no other high school in the area has a similar facility as it would most likely be too expensive for any school to build these days. The Max is the gym where Goodland student athletes, including Brook and Michele played basketball games and where Michele played volleyball.

Just ten days prior to 4,000 people sitting so quietly and mourning Brook in this facility, Brook and some of his football teammates from Nebraska were greeted with excitement and lots of cheers at The Max to play in a basketball exhibition game for the community. People in the Goodland community formed a team for the exhibition game and played against them. Brook and his teammates were going from town to town around different areas, mainly in Nebraska, playing these exhibition games in various communities. Michele did not go to this game but as she puts it, "Looking back on it now I can see that this exhibition basketball game kind of served as a final 'goodbye' for people in the community to see Brook before he passed away. People in Goodland still consider him a hometown hero.

"The day after his funeral I was walking through the smaller gym at our high school from one class to another."

Michele remembers, "I was walking with my best friend, Kelli Burr Carney, and I asked her if anything from the funeral affected her. I told her it really affected me, I felt God calling me.

"Brook passed away in April. That summer I had a waitressing job for about three weeks; it was hard to have a job and train for my upcoming freshman year of collegiate volleyball, so I didn't keep the job long. Later with some of that money I had earned I bought a Bible from the local bookstore in Goodland. I had my name embossed on the cover. It was special to have."

After a period of time trying to read her Bible and attending church services Michele found that there were occasions when she would be at church and people would say, "you remember the story about ....;" then they would go on and expand on that story. Michele began to realize, "No, I don't know that story."

It was at that point that Michele, a freshman in college and future Academic All-American, made an unusual decision. She decided to go to a Christian bookstore in Wichita, Kansas and purchase two children's Bibles.

"I wanted to be able to better understand some of the more familiar Bible stories. That is why I sought out those children's Bibles." Michele still has at least one of those Bibles.

About three years later, during the summer of 1999 before the start of Michele's senior year of college, Josh Ivans came to Wichita State to interview for the graduate assistant position with the women's volleyball program. Josh, like Michele, had grown up playing volleyball and after playing volleyball in college he decided to go into coaching. After the interview process ended another person was offered the position and took it, however near the start of the season the other applicant chose to take a different opportunity and that opened up the door for Josh to be hired. Over the course of the season Josh and Michele developed a good coach/player relationship and then after the season was over, they started dating.

"I grew up in a Christian home with a father whose love for Jesus and others was obvious," Josh recalls. "It was clear from as far back as I can remember that God was at the center of who he was. His profession from the time I was five years old was to work for a church so I saw him interact and love on so many different people in so many different ways. Also, he always extended that love to me and the rest of my family. He was patient, fair, fun, loving, kind, funny...the biggest hero and role model of my life this side of Heaven.

"I really wanted to model the life of my father, but I was missing the key ingredient - a true personal relationship with Christ. When I was in my junior year of college, and living a pretty messy life, I was on the phone with my dad. He was talking me through some things...he didn't know it but I was crying. I was listening...and I remember very clearly thinking about my dad, 'This can't be made up. This man is different...Jesus has to be real.' And so, I told Jesus I wanted him in my life, and wanted what my dad had. And from there, I put some effort into understanding what it meant to be a Christian. I still made lots of mistakes and I still make mistakes today, but I have been changed and growing ever since."

Over time Josh and Michele's relationship continued to evolve and it soon became clear to them that it was a part of God's plan for the two of them to be together.

Michele graduated in 2000, and then on June 2, 2001 Michelle and Josh were married. After college Michele went on to physical therapy school. Then December 2005 their first child, a daughter, Brooklan, was born. After coaching stints at Wichita State University, The University of Oklahoma, Louisiana State University, and Barton County Community College, Josh decided to move out of coaching so he would have more time to spend with his family. Later in the fall of 2007 Josh and Michele chose to move to Spring Hill, Kansas, and then in October of 2009 their second daughter, Ailiana, was born.

Later in the spring of 2014 Michele and Josh were expecting their third child, another daughter, Avelyn. As Michele's pregnancy progressed into her 28th week their doctors began doing a weekly ultrasound on Avelyn as a precaution because Michele was carrying extra amniotic fluid. Near the 32nd week the doctors found fluid on Avelyn's lungs.

On May 7, 2014 Avelyn KayLee Grace was born with hypertrophic cardiomyopathy, an enlarged heart. Josh, Michele and their family prayed, their friends prayed, and they expected Avelyn to live a fully functional life. Michele says, "I constantly prayed, 'God heal her, please heal her, just heal her God, I know you can heal her...' He did heal her, but not in the way I wanted. After just 16 short days of life, Avelyn went to heaven into the arms of Jesus."

After Avelyn passed away, even in the midst of their grief, they were determined to witness their faith in Christ. It was then that Josh and Michele made the selfless decision to use the money gifted to them as Avelyn's memorials to begin – what they would later call – Avelyn SonShine Journey, a ministry where they could share their story and the message of hope found in a relationship with Jesus Christ.

At first, they were not sure where to go with their ministry mission. With the help of their friends, Pete and Jennifer Nelson, who created the logo they still use; they made some bookmarks with their story on them and gave them away. They also started a website and shared their faith story, www.letyourlight-shine.com. And they bought some t-shirts for their oldest daughter, Brooklan's running club at Wolf Creek Elementary School and put their ministry website on the back of the shirts.

A few months later in October 2014, Michele and Brooklan went with the Wolf Creek running club to Hillsdale, Kansas to participate in a 5K Run. It was later decided this would be the Nathan Project's last 5K fundraiser running event.

Before the race began Michele met Ron Stiles and briefly shared her story. Michele and Brooklan then participated in the run. After the race ended Ron sought out Michele and told her he remembered hearing her story from his office manager, Diana Sowers, who just so happens to go to Michele's church, Life Spring Church in Spring Hill. Ron went on to tell Michele that he had been praying for Michele and her family.

As Michele and Ron talked after the run, Michele told Ron they still had memorial funds from Avelyn's memorial service and they had not decided what to do with the majority of the money. Michele told Ron they wanted two things to happen with the remaining memorial funds. First, they wanted to do something that would make a positive impact on others, and secondly, they wanted whatever they chose to be long-lasting - not just a one-time donation to a great cause.

About a week later Michele and Josh stopped by their church on a Saturday so Michele could run in to get something she needed to prepare for teaching preschool Sunday school the next day. While in the church Michele saw Ron's cousin, Keith Stiles, and Keith asked Michele if she had gotten a voicemail from Ron. Michele had not checked her phone's voicemail in a few days so when she got back into their van, she checked her messages and there on the voicemail was a message from Ron. Ron asked, "What about children's Bibles?" "Immediately Josh and I loved the idea...and after praying about it we felt like this was where God was leading us!" Michele said.

Ron told Michele and Josh he often got requests for children's Bibles but he didn't have any, so he thought that might be a good idea for their ministry. Josh recalls his first memory of Ron before they met was of seeing Ron speaking on television after Nathan had died.

"Ron was smiling and he genuinely looked happy," Josh remembers. "At the time I was thinking, 'Wow, that guy is different because he has just lost his son and he is on television smiling.' So, before Michele even met Ron, I already had an impression of him because I knew his story and I knew he was a Christian. He had already made an impact on me because of his faith, so when Michele met Ron and he later approached her after the Nathan Project race wanting to support us; it was not a surprise to me. And it felt good to be involved with someone with that kind of faith."

Once Josh and Michele decided on gifting away children's Bibles, Ron said he would have the company he uses for the Nathan Project Bibles, Bibles by the Case, send them samples of some children's Bibles to choose from. Before they got them, Josh and Michele were hoping there would be one in the samples like they had bought for Brooklan years earlier and there was. "I think there were three samples," Michele recalled, "but we immediately knew which one we wanted, the one we had been reading to our two older daughters for years."

"One of the things we love about the Nathan Project Bible," Michele continues, "is that it has Nathan's story in the front and back covers of the Bible. We feel having his story in the Bible can be really impactful. It took us a while to write what we wanted to be included about Avelyn's story in the children's Bibles. I wrote what I thought needed to be included and then Josh said he thought there should be something in the story about the age of accountability because Nathan was old enough to confess his faith whereas Avelyn was so young she couldn't."

"I felt like it was important that if we were going to claim that Avelyn was in heaven that we ought to back that up with scripture," Josh said. "So as part of our story I wanted to include that. The scripture talks about how there is a time in life called the 'age of accountability' when you are able to decide for yourself what you believe. When you lose a child that is only 16 days old, they clearly never got to that point so what happens to those people?"

As they were writing their story, Michele remembered a conversation she had a few years earlier with a newly Christian woman, Meghan Boehm, whom she had been mentoring at church. She had told Michele about a sermon she heard preached in their church that brought her peace about if a baby dies, they can go to heaven. Michele says, "as it often goes with teaching or mentoring, she taught me as much, if not more, than I was teaching her." Michele had not heard that sermon herself but she remembered their conversation, so she reached out to their pastor, Paul Sterrett, and he sent Josh and Michele his notes from his sermon. Those sermon notes helped Josh and Michele find the right scriptures that spoke to the 'exceptional mercy' God grants to those who are not of age to confess their faith. They were able to include this in their story, hoping these scripture verses might grant peace to someone who may have questions about the certainty of salvation for children who die before reaching the age of accountability.

"I am glad that we have Avelyn's story in the Bible," Josh continues, "because I think it is another way to draw people closer to God. But I also think it would be awesome one day if people start asking us questions about how we got started in our ministry and they have no idea that Avelyn was even a part of it because it becomes something bigger than her story, it becomes sharing the gospel with people.

"Sometimes people say to us 'thank you so much for what you are doing,' or 'thank you so much for the Bible,' and yet this is not really us. We are just facilitating what God is doing. When people give money to the ministry, they are the ones spreading the Gospel. Our hope is that everyone will come to know how much Jesus loves them and that those who have suffered loss know that God loves them, and that those who have questions and are searching know that Jesus loves them too.

"For me I had a lot of perspective change on what you hope for in life and a lot of opportunity to think about what is really important. And now that Avelyn is already in Heaven that is what we hope for all of our kids someday, that they would go to Heaven, and what a blessing it is for us to know she is already there. I think over time emotion changes, I don't have nearly as many days when I am sad and it is a blessing to grow closer to God. I definitely feel that my faith grew and the way I pray changed through this process. My response to God's answer to prayers changed through this process too. It can be frustrating when we pray for something and we don't get the answer we hoped for but there is a sense of peace involved when we don't get those answers and still have understanding that God has control over that situation and has a plan for it. So, my faith has grown through that and the fact that we will get to be with Avelyn someday is something I am very much looking forward to."

Once their story was written and the process of ordering the Bibles was complete the distribution phase began. In the beginning there were good days and bad days. But as time passed Josh and Michele began to see God at work in their ministry, and when there were times where they were not sure what to do or even what to hope for, Ron was there, supporting and encouraging them, to help them along their way.

The publisher for these Bibles is only able to have the inside covers custom printed by the manufacturer if it's an order of 2,500 Bibles or more. So, with their first few orders being less than 2,500 Bibles Josh and Michele had to print stickers with their story and place them in each Bible themselves. "Ron introduced us to his friend, Ben Manning," Michele said, "who worked for a printing company. He printed all these labels for us and donated the majority of them, which was a huge blessing to us especially in the beginning. It was a slow process putting in all the labels, but it was worth it."

A couple of years after Avelyn had passed away Michele was having a down day and she received a letter in the mail from an acquaintance, Diana Roth. In the letter she was thanking Michele for her Bible for her daughter, telling Michele how she had gotten it from Ron when he was in her office, and letting her know how much it meant to her. Ron always keeps at least one children's Bible in his truck to give away when/where needed. Michele and Josh learned this from him and now keep a box of children's Bibles in each vehicle. Now when they feel a tug on their hearts for a family that they think could use a Bible, they have them with them to gift away. Their kids enjoy doing this too. Their church also gives them away at child dedication services. They give away entire cases sometimes to various vacation Bible school programs in their area. Youth mission trips will take some of the Bibles with them and gift them away on their trips. Where God leads them, they give them away.

In the beginning Josh and Michele were not sure who they were going to give the Bibles to or how they were going to do it. But over time God has provided.

"Ron helped us with the task of deciding who to give the Bibles to," Michele said. "When we first started our ministry it wasn't taking off like we wanted it to, so Ron came over and he shared that he had gotten to a similar place in their ministry and he had to just turn it over to the Lord and say, 'God this is yours so you take it where you want it to go.' That was a big encouragement to me because I was sort of holding onto the Bibles because we only had so many and Ron encouraged me to begin giving them to anyone when I felt that tug on my heart because God will provide. So, this really helped me.

"God has walked along our journey with us to keep this ministry going. The main way He has kept Avelyn SonShine Journey going allowing us to order more Bibles," Michele says, "is by holding our Annual Let Your Light Shine Family 1 Mile & 5K with a silent auction. Our friends Tim and Sharon Meek helped us get this going initially as well as our friend, Amber Miller, who has helped us year after year. We could not do this without the help of our friends, family and community.

"We have multiple monetary sponsors who are so generous! Businesses and individuals from the Spring Hill area and from across the United States who donate in person, through the mail and on our website to support our ministry. Besides monetary donations, some give items for our silent auction. Family, the weekend of, and volunteers, the day of, give their time and talents to make the event a success. And many of our friends, family and even strangers participate and support our 5K Run and 1 Mile Family Walk. This past May 2019 marked the 5th annual event.

"It's so much work to put all this together, but every year we feel so blessed and humbled by the support we receive, we feel surrounded by so much love. To God be the Glory! He has taken this ministry places we never imagined.

"Shortly after Avelyn passed away I made an album for her," Michele recalls. "At the time we had put the bookmark together, but we still did not know what we were going to do with the majority of her memorial funds. Before the thought of children's Bibles had ever entered our minds, on the back of Avelyn's album – by a picture of the bookmark – I wrote, 'We hope to continue to encourage others ~ by God's Grace~ by sharing your story. This bookmark is the start to what we hope will be big things.'

"We are so thankful God has walked with us along this journey and strengthened our faith as we have seen and experienced these 'big things' more than we could have ever dreamed."

To date the Avelyn SonShine Journey has ordered over 6,000 Children's Bibles. God is definitely doing 'big things.'

In addition to their Bible ministry, Avelyn SonShine Journey, in recent years Josh and Michele have also started a sports ministry, SonShine Athletic Academy.

Josh's coaching experience and their shared background as college athletes made it a natural fit for them to begin working in sports ministry, specifically volleyball, as a way to reach young people and their parents with the gospel message through organizing and hosting volleyball clinics.

With Josh and Michele both juggling the responsibility of work and family – including the addition of a son, Andersen, in 2016, life is busy. But with their talents in athletics and their heart for ministry it is easy to imagine numerous ways that God could open the door for the Ivan's to combine their passions for volleyball and for sharing their testimonies into a powerful ministry.

"Sports is such a magnet for young people," Josh continued, "and we have talked about how cool it would be to combine with other people whom we know that are coaches and have faith based clinics for different sports but only God knows what He has planned for this.

"I try and use the talents that I believe God gave me in many ways," Josh declared. "I am always thinking of new ways to teach/coach and reach people, so who knows where it will lead. There are a lot of people hungry for knowledge and skill, so I'll keep teaching and coaching where it seems to make the most sense. I also find that God will reveal abilities in areas you don't expect, if you pray for that - again, simply asking God to lead my steps. I never dreamed I would be able to speak in front of large groups when I was in college, but I do it all the time now."

Michele and Josh are thankful for the support and inspiration that they have found in Ron and the Nathan Project and as the years have passed their relationship has become closer as they all work together to share the message of the Gospel through their ministries by gifting away the Bibles.

"We have a dedication sticker in the front of the Bibles and the stickers read; 'The Avelyn SonShine Journey in conjunction with The Nathan Project'," Michele said, "We feel God has a way to make things happen, and it did happen the way God wanted, He used Ron as the avenue to speak to us. Ron told us, that it wasn't his idea, it was the Holy Spirit that used him to say to us, 'What about children's Bibles?' Ron will be the first to say it wasn't him, God gave him the words to speak to us."

"Ron has a heart for service," Josh continues, "God has placed that on his heart and Ron just responds. The fact that he went and approached Michele after the Nathan Project 5k was over and saying to her 'Hey I do remember your story,' and then taking the time to get involved and then meeting with us at our house personally on more than one occasion. He is willing as a servant to respond to what the Holy Spirit is telling him. And that's huge, that's how things grow, that's how the Gospel gets spread."

"It wasn't until recently that I have really thought much about the 'process' with all this," Michele said, "from Brook's death and his memorial service leading me to become a Christian and later me seeking out a children's Bible to read myself. Then meeting Ron at the Nathan Project 5k and telling him our story and hopes and afterward Ron reaching out and calling me a week later suggesting children's Bibles as he told us, 'The Holy Spirit told me to tell you.' Then Bibles by the Case sending us a sample of the same Bible we had been reading to our two older daughters for years. It is quite the series of events. Only God could ordain this."

But that's not the end of their story. God has made Josh and Michele's mission, with their Avelyn SonShine Journey, to get children's Bibles into the hands of as many children and families as possible. They feel God has called them, along with many others who support them in their ministry, to be the hands and feet to get, as they feel called, these children's Bibles into the hands of God's children.

"We have heard some stories of how much kids/families appreciate the children's Bibles and it does my heart so much good," Michele continues, "but it will be fun, amazing, beautiful, and humbling to one day hear how God has used these Bibles in the lives of so many.

"Praise God for handling all this and working all things for good."

Romans 8:28 *"And we know that in all things God works for the good of those who love Him, who have been called according to His purpose."*

35

It was a Friday night in the fall of 2014 in Olathe, Kansas, just a short ten-minute ride north up Hwy 169 from Spring Hill, Kansas, where during a high school football game between Olathe East and Olathe South High Schools, Olathe East senior linebacker James McGinnis made what appeared to be a routine tackle on an Olathe South ball carrier. However, during the play that looked like a typical tackle you would see any Friday night in a high school football game, James suffered a subdural hematoma, bleeding of the brain. Within a matter of moments emergency responders were on the field treating and then quickly transporting James to nearby Overland Park Regional Medical Center where doctors performed emergency surgery removing a part of James' skull to relieve the pressure on James' brain, saving his life.

After surgery James remained motionless in a coma for five days. On the fifth day the doctors told James' parents, Pat and Susan McGinnis, that it was okay for them to go into his room and talk to him, but if the pressure on his brain goes up, they would have to back off. Later one day as Pat was standing on James' right side and Susan was on James' left side as they were holding his hands, telling him that they loved him and they were proud of him, James moved the middle finger and ring finger of his right hand, bringing them into his palm signaling to his parents the 'I love you' sign.

The "I love you' sign started for James in kindergarten. When his parents would drop him off at school it was a way without shouting across the playground at school to signal, we love you. That was the only sign language they knew, was the 'I love you sign.'

When James came out of the coma, he couldn't open his eyes, he couldn't talk. The only way he could communicate was by moving the fingers on his right hand, and he did it, he shared the I love you sign with his parents.

"It was so special to us," Susan remembers, "because up until that point the doctors had told us that he was probably going to be in a vegetative state. So, when he moved the fingers on his hand and signaled the 'I love you sign', that told us that number one he heard us, number two he understood us, and number three he was responding back to us. So, for me, seeing that told me, he is in there, he is going to be okay."

It was during those first few days while James was in the ICU that a mutual friend of the McGinnis' reached out to Ron and Connie Stiles to set up a meeting with them and the McGinnis'. And as has been their usual response over the years whenever someone in need had reached out for support, Ron and Connie showed up.

"We met Ron and Connie during the first five days when James was in ICU and we couldn't talk to James or interact with him, or touch him or do anything to stimulate him," Pat said, "and during that time the media was just crazy reporting on what had happened to James and also bringing up old stories in the news, including Nathan's story. So, I started to have survivors' guilt, knowing that those families were having a hard time, having to relive those memories.

"We were so blessed when they came up and visited." Pat continued, "That is when we initially started sharing stories about James and Nathan. It was really cool to hear so many similarities the two of them shared. Sometimes we are asked today, 'How do you and Susan do it?' We are still going through recovery with James 4 and ½ years later, and my first response is always, 'well I still have the opportunity to talk to James. If you want to see a model of how you deal with adversity, it is Ron and Connie, who have taken this tragedy and turned it into a positive with their ministry.' Their love of God and Christ is definitely shining through when you look at their ministry work and see how they have turned Nathan's story into a very positive inspirational message for everyone."

Susan says that when Ron and Connie came to the hospital, the first time she met them, they didn't know what was going to happen with James. James was still alive, but at that point they didn't know for how long. With all the bad news they kept getting from the doctors they did not know what to expect. "And in walks this set of parents, and I was just in awe of their strength and how they were handling it. It set a good example for Pat and me, that no matter what we were going to be facing, whether it was a long rehab, or whether we were going to be planning a funeral we can get through this. That was the first thing I noticed about them. Then the more that we shared the similarities between our two kids, I knew that our meeting was meant to be. It just helped us in so many ways, on so many different levels, and to watch what they have done with Nathan's legacy, it is beautiful."

"When Ron and Connie first came into the hospital, they were there to comfort us, but they had been on my mind and so I had the opportunity to ask them to tell me about Nathan," Pat recalls. "To hear Ron, speak about Nathan and to hear him tell me about Nathan, you could see the similarities between Nathan and James were definitely there. They were both very family oriented; they were both very close to their sisters. How both James and Nathan loved sports, how much joy they had from playing sports, how they lived and breathed it, but that sports did not take over either of their lives. And their goofy sense of humor, and what a goofball Nathan could be, and how funny and silly and fun he was, that definitely could be James."

One of the things the McGinnis' learned when they met Ron and Connie was that Nathan had other brothers and sisters, and that one of them, Josie Stiles, was a teacher where

James went to school at Olathe East High School. The next time they had parent teacher conferences James was still in rehab and Pat went in to meet with his teachers. After Pat finished speaking with James' teachers, he felt compelled to go and introduce himself to Josie. Pat told Josie, "'you guys are in our prayers, we are praying for peace and we hope that this doesn't bring up too many bad memories for you.' She was so supportive and encouraging to us. Josie is a wonderful person."

Later on, when the opportunity came for Josie and James to meet, from the very first moment they were like kindred spirits. Even though James never had Josie for a teacher, they have this bond that is there. It is the same with Ron and Connie and Pat and Susan; the two families share this connection too. Pat says it was almost like they were this family that you know you have but you have been separated from for a while, and when they saw them, they just picked up where they left off, and yet they had never met.

"I think going through a tragedy like this, or adversity I would say," Pat continues, "has a tendency to create a bond among people who have experienced similar events, and part of that bond is highlighting what is important in life. It's not about whether you get to a certain place on time, it's more about those friendships, the interactions you have day to day with people, and the sacrifices you make for others. When you go through those kinds of shared experiences it does have a way of changing your outlook on life."

"I think sometimes focusing on others, which is what Ron and Connie have done," says Susan, "takes the focus off of your grief, which is always there, it is not going to go away, and you see that there are a lot of people out there who have struggles. It helps you re-channel that energy in a positive way, and that's what I see in Connie and Ron, to not focus on their own grief but to help other families."

While James was in a comma, Pat and Susan along with their family and friends were continually praying for James. It was during this time when some of the kids who were friends of James approached Susan saying, "We want to do something, we want to do something," and Pat and Susan told them, "pray, pray, pray." Finally, one of the kids said, 'I want to do something real."

So, Susan explained to the kids, "that when you are up in the hospital, up in the ICU, it's a cold, dark, ugly place, and you are surrounded by death. That's what you see there, but your prayers are making a difference for us."

When James was small Susan would tell James whenever he would have a nightmare, to not be afraid and they would say a prayer together. They would ask God to send his angel armies to protect James. And James would go back off to sleep, because even in his childlike faith, he knew there were angels in the room protecting him. Therefore, Susan told these kids, "it really is true when you say these prayers, then we are feeling those angel armies in James' room. I told the kids who were praying for James, 'When you walk into James' room it is peaceful, it was beautiful, and that is through the power of your prayers.'"

Susan remembers there would be times during James stay in the hospital when she and Pat would be in the room with James while he was still in the comma, and nurses would walk in and take a deep breath, exhale and walk out. They could feel the peace that was present in James' room. "That is what it felt like," Susan says, "and it came from the power of prayer from those kids and everyone else in the city who was praying for James."

After James' injury, while he was still in the hospital recovering, the hallways of his school were lined with 'Pray for James' posters. "All the kids and teachers in the school witnessed that," Pat recalled. "During those first few days the doctors did not give James much of a chance of surviving, and then when the students and others in their community saw James come through, it changed their outlook on their own faith. There have been several of James' friends who after seeing this happen to James decided to go into the ministry and some into occupational therapy, physical therapy or nursing to help others. Witnessing James' injury and recovery changed their outlook and perspective on what is important.

"James has three Bible verses that he wakes up to on his mirror every morning and one of them is about courage, it is Joshua 1:9. (NLT)

"This is my command—be strong and courageous! Do not be afraid or discouraged. For the Lord your God is with you wherever you go."

"That is the same verse that Ron and Connie chose to put on Nathan's gravesite," Pat exclaimed. "That verse talks about having faith and courage because God is always with you, that we are not to fear, so that is how James has chosen to live his life. I know this, had Nathan and James met there is no doubt they would have been best friends."

Before his injury, whenever James was playing sports, he would wear an Under Armour shirt under his jersey with 'Philippians 4:13' printed on the back and the verse written below it: *"For I can do everything through Christ, who gives me strength."* (NLT)

James did this as a way to quietly witness his faith to his teammates. So, when he took his pads off everyone could see it.

James says today that he has learned that you have to focus on the now, not tomorrow or the past, because with God in your life, He will control your future, and He will have many plans for you. But it might take four or five years to get to doing what you want to.

Later in the winter of 2014 there was another event that linked Nathan, James and their families together.

The Simone Awards, an awards program to recognize the most outstanding high school football players in the greater Kansas City metropolitan area, established the Nathan Stiles Inspiration Award in 2010. This award is given annually in memory of Nathan, to recognize a person at the Simone Awards banquet who has been involved in high school football and demonstrated the high qualities and values Nathan stood for. Someone whose life has been an inspiration to those who know them and is representative of the positive influence Nathan had on the many people his life impacted.

In 2014, the 4th Annual Nathan Stiles Inspiration Award was given to James McGinnis. "The Nathan Stiles Inspiration Award was greatly timed as far as motivation for James," Pat said.

"When I received the Nathan Stiles Inspiration Award that was a big motivation for me," James stated. "It motivated me to keep going, it let me know you've got this. It was just a huge blessing for me to receive that award."

When the time came for the Simone Awards banquet to be held, James was still in the hospital so he couldn't be there to receive the award. The Simone Awards committee made the decision to have a film crew come up to the hospital and film James. They played that film at the Simone Awards banquet. Pat attended the ceremony and accepted the award on James' behalf along with four of his teammates from the football team.

Later in the school year once James was out of the hospital and back at school, they had an awards ceremony for the graduating senior class on Awards Day. That senior night, Nathan's sister, Josie Stiles, presented James with the award in front of his school. As Pat says, "That was a special night."

"When I presented the award to James, I was so incredibly happy that James was well enough to walk across the stage and accept the award at his own high school, the school where I had the privilege of teaching," Josie recalls. "Although, I had never had James in class it felt as though I had known him forever.

"James can look at a crowd of people and one person stands out to him. He will engage that person in a conversation and before you know it, he is hearing their story and encouraging them. He came in my class one day to tell me hello, and he told his story to the class and they saw his incredible attitude in the midst of the hard work he has to continually do to keep his progress/healing moving forward. The kids were so encouraged by him and it seemed they felt that they could fight the hard things and push through them the way James does. They talked about him for days.

"Nathan's platform for God looks different than James' but they both move others closer to Jesus by the life they chose to live. Not many people leave a legacy in their fully lived life compared to what Nathan and James have in their first two decades. Simple choices of looking into the eyes of others, valuing them as God's handiwork, and loving Jesus by loving others without a disclaimer is how they each live/lived."

The year after James had recovered enough to speak, the Simone Awards asked James if he would like to do an acceptance speech. The Simone Awards that year was being held at the same high school where Ron had been asked earlier to come and speak to the volleyball team. When the coaches ask Ron to come speak, they told Ron that they would love to have him but if he was going to be talking about the faith aspect of Nathan's story the school would not allow them to have him. Ron told the coaches that if he could not talk about faith then he could not come and talk about Nathan because faith is a big part of his story. This time though, when it came time for James to be honored and address the people at the awards ceremony, James would be speaking at this school not just to the volleyball team, but to the whole student body. And that particular year the winners of the inspiration award were firemen who had lost their lives battling a fire in Kansas City.

James began his speech by thanking the community for all of the love and support they had given him, and he thanked the rescue responders who told him he was 'in God's hands that night.' Then James told them that, "they were God's hands and feet that night when they cared for him, because they got him to the hospital in time." He encouraged the student body by telling them, "when you help others you too can be God's hands here on earth."

You could have heard a pin drop that night during James whole presentation. Since then he has gone on to do several other events where he has given his testimony in front of large groups of people. James is now asked to go and speak in high schools where he shares his faith and an anti-bullying message, that we should love one another.

That first night when James went up in front of the assembly to speak there were over 1000 kids there in attendance. When James came off the stage that night Pat said to James, "Before the injury you could not have gotten up and spoken like that in front of four people."

James says that his dad is right; he could not have gotten up in front of a group and spoken like that before the injury. "But it is like I told my mom and dad that night," James says, "Once you have faced death the way I have, what is there to be afraid of?"

Susan says being recognized as the Nathan Stiles Inspiration Award winner was a huge honor for James. Winning the award also became a stepping stone for James to realize that he now had this platform that was given to him by Nathan, Ron and Connie to go and speak to people. Discovering that James had this newfound gift to share his testimony was a gift given to him which allowed James and his family to see that James could go and speak in front of groups, sharing his story and his faith.

"The Stiles family, they are like family to us now," says Pat. "They are that close. We only see them about three or four times a year, but it is like we have known each other our whole lives. We see them at the Simone Awards each year now because James is always asked to come back and present the Nathan Stiles Inspiration Award."

James' mission now is to go out and speak to individuals and groups and tell his story. Often times when people he speaks to hear his story they will break down into tears and say something like, 'You don't know how much I needed to hear that today.'

James often tells the story of a trip the family took to Little Rock, Arkansas a few years ago. They were traveling by car, and they stopped at a gas station and there was a group of bikers parked in the parking lot. James told Susan he wanted to go up and talk to these bikers. At first Pat and Susan were fearful for James but he persisted. So, James and Pat went over to the group of bikers and James shared his story with them. He told them to love one another. *(John 13:34)* *"A new command I give you: love one another. As I have loved you, so you must love one another."* Before James had finished, nearly all of the people in this biker group, these large burley men, were in tears, and one man told James and Pat, 'You do not know how much I needed to hear that, I was abused as a child.'

James lives his life like that today. Whenever James feels God tugging on his heart to reach out to someone he goes forward and shares his story. James says that goes back to the Bible verse both James and Nathan loved, Joshua 1:9, *'be strong and courageous, for your God is with you wherever you go.'*

There have been times since the injury when Susan and Pat would ask James why he would stop and pick people in what appeared to be a random coincidence to go and speak to? One day Susan asked James why he had approached a particular man at a bookstore while they were standing in line waiting to check out, and James said to her, 'Couldn't you see the pain in his eyes.'

"Sometimes I think the one-on-one encounters are more powerful than speaking in front of large groups." Susan continues, "But either way, however it happens James is a man on a mission, to spread Jesus' message to love one another. That is James' way of witnessing. And the cool thing is with the Nathan Project, Nathan's legacy is sharing God's word with hundreds of people all over the world through the Bibles. So, they are both kind of doing the same thing. It just leads back to the fact that Nathan's story did not end in his death, and it's not going to end, because the impact from the Nathan

Project ministry will live on in the lives of the people it has touched forever.

"I believe James is attuned now to the still small voice of the Holy Spirit. I believe James listens for that voice, and when he hears the Holy Spirit speak to him, telling him to go up and speak to someone, he does it. That's what I believe it is," said Susan.

When James is asked how this experience has changed his faith he says, "What's weird about it is that it hasn't changed my faith, it's just that after this experience, now I know that there is a God and Jesus. It's just an amazing feeling."

36

John Manning was seven years old when he began losing his eyesight. John says the doctors told his parents when his vision problems began that his vision would continue to deteriorate to a point and then level off, and by the time he was twelve years old his vision would stabilize, and his vision would stay at that level of blindness for the rest of his life. Between the ages of seven and twelve, as John's vision continued to decrease, he became more and more self-conscious about the loss of his eyesight, and as a result of that, John began to withdraw from other kids his own age and isolate himself. John remembers that during those childhood years, he was at home alone a lot, and as a result of his insecurities and isolation he became very attached to his mother.

"My dad was a brick mason who owned his own business. He worked hard and he did not want his son to become a mama's boy, so he began to take me to his jobsites on the weekends and during the summer when I was twelve years old, to work with his masonry crews. He did the best he could as he helped me learn how to function with my bad eyesight. The summer before my thirteenth birthday, I worked with my dad's masonry crew every day that entire summer. I worked 60-70 hours a week, all summer long. I gained a lot of muscle mass working for my dad that summer, and I became very good at moving bricks and mixing masonry cement.

"My dad was a good man, but he had his struggles too. He was a functioning alcoholic, and he also was a workaholic. He had a policy while we were at work that no employee could drink before 2:30 in the afternoon. That summer since I was working like a man, he let me drink with the men. Working with the men that summer and seeing that I could work and do a good job gave me some confidence in myself, and after that summer I felt I was ready to fit in with other kids."

Unfortunately for John, his experience of drinking on the jobsite with his dad's construction crew that summer was about to lead him down a road to addiction.

"I sought out the kids that were drinking because I enjoyed drinking. By age 13 I had been introduced to marijuana. I had been working all summer so I had some money that most other kids did not have, so I quickly went from smoking marijuana to selling it so I could support my habit. A lot of people who use drugs will also sell drugs to support their addictions. It was my drug habit that started me into the world of selling drugs as a 13-year-old.

"When I was a young kid in school, being legally blind, where we lived, there weren't any special education classes available for blind kids like we have today. When I was a kid in school back then in the 1960's, if you were suffering from blindness you either went to the school for blind children in St. Louis, Missouri, or you sat in public school classrooms and learned as much as you could from listening to the teacher, because as a blind child you cannot read the textbooks. So, I learned how to learn by listening."

As a result of John's vision impairment and the limited educational opportunities available to him in public school, his parents decided that it would be okay for him to quit school and do construction work full time with his father's masonry company at age 15. "They were thinking that I could work in construction work the rest of my life. The eye doctors told my parents that my eyesight would remain the same from then on, and it did up until the time I was 29 years old. Then as the years passed my vision problems became worse.

"At the point when I quit school and started working full time, my dad told my mom that since I was working full time that I was a man now, and I was allowed to drink at home. This escalated my alcoholism because I no longer had to hide it," said John.

By the time John was 15 years old his drug habit had grown to the point where he was doing speed and some other drugs as well.

"Speed allowed me to drink all I wanted without getting drunk."

When John was 18 years old, he was still heavily addicted to and selling marijuana and other pills like speed. It was during this year that John was involved in an accident at work.

"I fell and landed on a pile of bricks. After the accident I was bedridden for quite a while, and I could not work for several months. As a result of that injury I was given muscle relaxers and pain pills. I was already an alcoholic at that time, and I soon realized that if I took those pain pills and drank alcohol with them, it was a totally different high. So, once the prescription for the pain pills ran out, I began seeking out other people who had those kinds of prescription drugs and would buy them from people who had them. From there I became a pill addict as well."

As was the case with the other drugs, John says he would buy the drugs in volume and use what he needed, then he would sell the rest of the drugs so he could make money and have his for free.

"Sometime later as I was taking and selling pills someone introduced me to valium and valium was the most intense high, I had ever been on. I started out drinking whiskey and taking valiums. At first it was two or three pills at a time, then a couple of years later I got up to 20 or 30 pills a day. At that point, even as an addict, I realized I had developed a severe drug problem."

By this time John had been married and divorced once, and was in his second marriage where he had a stepdaughter and two children who he fathered with his second wife. As his addictions grew, his life was spiraling out of control. But even in the midst of his addiction, his relationship with his children was beginning to soften John's heart, and he realized he was not the father his children needed him to be. John decided that his children needed to be involved in church. Even though he did not attend church himself, he sought out a place for them to go so they could be exposed to some Christian education, something that John did not have himself as a child.

"I was not raised in a Christian home so I did not have exposure to the Bible as a child," says John. "I sent my kids to Sunday school when they were two and three years old because I knew they needed to go, that it was important, but I did not go myself until years later."

During that time even though John's life was a mess and he was not at that time seeking God, John met someone who would become an important influence in his life.

"Vernon West's wife was my girl's Sunday school teacher, and even when I was dealing drugs and had a bad reputation in the neighborhood, Vernon was always nice to me. Vernon would invite me to go bowling with the group if my kids Sunday school class was going bowling and he would invite me to church when he would pick my kids up to take them to Sunday school. He never passed judgement on me, he is a pastor now, but he was not a pastor at that time, he was just a guy going to church. He was always kind to me, and his showing me kindness made an impact on me."

During this time as Vernon was visiting John at his home and reaching out to him, trying to help John to turn his life around and inviting him to church, there was someone from Vernon's church who told him that he should leave John alone because John was a bad person. This church member told Vernon they knew that John was dealing drugs, and that Vernon should not be going to see him. Vernon told this person that John was just a person who was making bad choices, and that he needed Jesus.

"That is what people who are believers need to realize," John continues, "that someone they see who is making bad choices is just someone who hasn't been introduced to Christ. They are just someone who has not yet chosen to take hold of the Word of God and let it mold them into the people they need to be. Vernon did an awesome job of setting an example of what a Christian should be by being kind to me. Even when I wasn't a very loveable person because of who I was, and the lifestyle I lived. I had one neighbor where I used to live who was a member of the church who was very unkind to me. When I was struggling with my lifestyle this person would say unkind things to me, and knowing he was going to church regularly I saw him as representative of who Christians were. The way this person spoke negatively to me and judged me for my drug problem and lifestyle issues was not a good example of how a Christian person should treat someone who is struggling with an addiction."

Still, even with Vernon's attempts to reach John, John's life continued to unravel as his addictions worsened and his relationship with his second wife and their homelife became more volatile.

"One night we were partying at a friend's house and I was really high," John recalls. "I got angry with my wife and I climbed in our car and took off. I was on such a high that I was still awake, but I had mentally blacked out, because I don't even remember doing it. Somehow as I was driving, I became alert enough that I sort of woke up, and I realized I was alone driving a car. I was alert enough then that I turned the car around and tried to drive back to my friend's house, but I wrecked, totaled the car and broke my nose. I was still high enough after the accident and breaking my nose that I somehow got out of the car and took the drugs I had with me out of my pocket and hid them next to a tree. Then I went up to someone's house and told them I had wrecked my car and asked for help.

"After that my wife told me that if I didn't quit the valiums, I would lose my kids. I quit the valiums but my alcoholism, drug addictions and dealing the other drugs continued."

Later when John was 29 years old, he suffered another accident at work, and this time it would begin a series of events that would transform his life.

"When I was 29 years old, I was working on some scaffolding and fell, and that injury required me to have elbow surgery and back surgery. After that I received disability and stayed home with my two kids and a stepdaughter. Over time I began to realize what kind of an influence my drug dealing was having on my kids and I decided that I needed to quit being a drug dealer, an addict and an alcoholic. So, I made the decision to give up that lifestyle and I moved away from my friends and the neighborhood I had been living in and moved out to the country in Bates County, Missouri. That was all done to help me get away from the drugs, and the people I sold drugs to. I changed my playmates and my playground.

"Soon thereafter my wife and I divorced and I got custody of our children when they were ages six and seven years old. That move and the divorce began a change in my lifestyle and I quit using and selling drugs, and I began to go to church. At that point I was not really seeking God; it was to make me look better as a single father who was trying to raise his children.

"I realized that I did not want to lose my kids, that was the motivation I needed to help me quit the drugs. At the time I thought it was me alone who did it, but now with all I know about the power of drug addiction, I believe it was God who helped me get off the drugs. A person just does not quit using drugs like that on their own, looking back I know now that God helped me to quit using drugs. I truly believe it was God who had His hand in taking away that addiction to the valium from me. Usually someone can't walk away from a valium addiction like I had on their own."

John says that the world of recovery from drugs is a slow process. In order to help people who are recovering from addictions you have to be patient with them and kind to them. If they mess up you can't go over and fuss at them and chew them out, you have to encourage them to get back up and try again. It's a lot like riding a bike, when you fall you have to get back up and go again. John says that a lot of people when they get clean for a while and they are trying to get off drugs, they will fall several times before they are totally able to quit. It's just part of the process of getting off drugs; the temptation level to relapse is really huge. John says he believes his recovery from drugs was made possible in large part because he chose to move away from everyone he knew before.

John believes strongly that the person who is using drugs or addicted to alcohol, in their minds while they are battling their demons of addiction, they do not realize how badly what they are doing to themselves is affecting other people, the people that love them and are depending on them. John says for him and many other recovering addicts, it takes seeing how their lifestyle choices are affecting others to give them the sense of purpose they need to get clean and change their lives.

John remembers that once he started attending church and he was exposed to God's Word; he began to see how the message of salvation through a relationship with Christ could change his life. "Learning about Jesus' teachings and listening to God's Word helped me deal with my divorce and the teachings of the Bible helped me raise my two daughters, and turn away from the lifestyle I had been living," declares John. "Soon I became very interested in the Word of God. In time I came to Christ, and I prayed that God would put someone in my life to help me raise my children. Soon thereafter I met my wife Angie. We got married when my girls were nine and ten years old, and she had a son that was seven and a daughter that was twelve."

"When I first met John," says Angie Manning, "I had custody of my two kids and I had been divorced for two years and I started going back to church. I was raised in a church, my mom took us to church, my dad didn't go but my mom did. And I got away from that, I got into the party life for a while and I didn't want my kids making the same mistakes I did. So, I thought, 'we are going to start going to church,' and once we began going to church God began working in me to change my life. He took those old desires away from me. Then a few months later, one day as I was sitting in church, I asked God to bring a man into my life again, to help me raise my kids. And then I thought about that and said, 'no God I'm just kidding, maybe I don't need a man now.' Then the very next weekend I met John. That was kind of a funny story.

"So, we took two families of three and made a family of six together. That same summer I had bought my kids a trampoline and he had bought his kids a trampoline too, so we had our kids playing on trampolines together, we had that in common too, that was kind of neat. We have been married 27 years now and we have beaten the odds because we are now in our third marriages, and statistically speaking we should have been divorced a long time ago. But I think what has made the difference is having God in our relationship. He is the center, the glue that holds us together."

"It wasn't long after I met Angie," says John, "that we found out that Vernon had become a pastor. I told Angie, 'if that man is a pastor, I would like to try his church,' and she agreed, so we started going to his church, and he is still our pastor today, almost 27 years later.

"When I first started attending Vernon's church whenever someone would come to Vernon with a drug problem, he would connect me with them because he knew drugs was a part of my past. Later, Vernon took some of us to a Promise Keepers ministry meeting in Arrowhead Stadium in Kansas City that was attended by 78,000 people. After attending that meeting, I began to have some confidence that I could serve in the ministry.

"I later became involved in the Children's Evangelists Fellowship where I was introduced to the *Wordless Book* story of salvation. While ministering in the Children's Evangelists Ministry, I began to realize that drug addicts and alcoholics gravitated to me for help. That was when other people began to tell me that my ministry was to help people who had addictions. Pastor Vernon always told me that helping people recover from addictions was my ministry because I had that in my past."

It was in October 2003 that John started a prison ministry in the Bates County jail. "I started to share the Bible with them, but at the time I really was not sure what I was doing. I went there to share my testimony with them and share the *Wordless Book* story of salvation. To tell them about the kind of person I used to be, and what God had done in my life.

"Having lived the lifestyle of an alcoholic, a drug addict and a dealer, and being able to share my recovery testimony helps me minister to addicts. I am able to tell them where I am at today and how much better my life is since I no longer have to deal with the things they are dealing with. When you're a drug addict or an alcoholic you are always looking over your shoulder for fear of being busted for selling to the wrong person. I'm lucky that I never got put in prison. I truly believe that God has always had as a part of His plan for my life, for me to be doing the ministry work I am doing today."

Another message that John strives to explain to people who are struggling with addiction or parents who are looking for ways to help their addicted children, is that in most cases addictions begin when people are either still children or during their teenage years.

"Addictions to drugs and alcohol starts early, normally as a party thing, a social choice children or teenagers make to be accepted as part of the group. They begin drinking and doing drugs because they are trying to fit in with the other kids, wanting to be a part of the party life." John continues, "Addiction is not a choice; it is a problem that begins when young people go down the road of wanting to drink or do drugs to be a part of the party lifestyle, and in most cases, the addiction accelerates as children become teenagers, and if not treated, becomes worse on into adulthood. Then most addicts will typically begin to sell drugs to support their habit. Once they begin to sell drugs, they not only become addicted to the drugs, but also the fast-easy money that comes from dealing. At that point, the addict has two problems, a drug addiction and a money problem, making their addictions even harder to overcome.

"In the little town we live in, Butler, Missouri, they have a small-town Baptist Church Association there, and there was a deacon in one of the churches in Butler, who has a son-in-law named Pat Apple. Pat is a close friend of Ron Stiles and a supporter of the Nathan Project. The pastor of the church began to tell me about the Nathan Project and that they were gifting away Bibles and he thought I should learn about it because of my work in the jail ministry. So, when I first learned about the Nathan Project, I hadn't met Ron or Pat, I had just talked to Pat over the phone. And from there Pat got me Bibles from the Nathan Project to use in the Bates County jail ministry. When I first began to get the Bibles from the Nathan Project, I gave them mostly to the younger men, ages 17 to early 20's. Then, as I learned more about Nathan and the ministry, I began to tell these young men Nathan's story, about the impact reading the Bible had made in his life, and also about the impact the Word of God had made in my life. Then I would bring the Nathan Project Bibles to the jail and give them to the people I was ministering to, and ask them to read the front and back cover, to see if they were willing to take that challenge, of reading the Bible every day, and letting the Word of God mold them. It was quite a while later that I actually got to meet Ron. When we met, Ron told me about his ministry work and how working in the prison ministry with Bill Corum and some of the people he had met through the Nathan Project had changed his life and that he felt this ministry was a call on his life that God has given to him, in the same way as the ministry God has given me to work with people who are recovering from addictions has changed my life."

"Over the years John and I have experienced quite a few tragedies in our lives together," Angie noted. "The biggest one was losing my daughter when she was 21 years old. She had gotten married and had two small children, three and four years old. She was killed in a car wreck coming home from work one day.

"Later one day after my daughter died, I was feeling so down about losing her. There were some circumstances after my daughter's death that made it appear that we may have very limited visitation with my grandchildren. As a result of that I was afraid that in addition to losing her, that I might also lose contact with my grandchildren. That same day John was in town and saw my granddaughter and her father, and after they talked, unbeknownst to me, he was able to bring the children by our home to visit me. As I was driving on my way home from work that day, I had cried out to God to please bring these kids back into my life. When I pulled up in our driveway and I saw those two little faces of my grandchildren looking out the window, I got out of my car and as fast as I could I ran to the house and they came running outside and I met them on the steps and we all screamed and hugged each other. I started crying, it was such a special answer to my prayer. Only God could do something like that. So, I know He is real, I know He works in people's lives.

"It was a God thing that John and I got together. At the very first it was rocky, because we had two families we were bringing together, and we had our trials we had to go through together.

"Oftentimes when people are suffering through tragedies, like when the Stiles lost Nathan, or when we lost our daughter, they turn away from God, which is so sad because that is when we need God the most. When your life is upside down, that relationship with God is what keeps you going.

"Ironically, one of the things that I think has been a huge blessing in the success of John's ministry," says Angie, "strangely enough, is his eyesight. That is, since John cannot see, he cannot look at somebody and judge them by what they look like, or the way they may appear to other people. I know I have been guilty of that at times, I have looked at somebody before and thought, 'Well I don't think you'll ever change,' because of who they appear to be or the trials they are experiencing. John is not that way; he is not judgmental. He likes to share his love of Jesus with just about everybody he meets."

Angie is currently working full time but she looks forward to the day when she can retire and help John more in his ministry work. She has recently begun to work alongside John ministering to the women in the Bates County jail, sharing her story and teaching them about Jesus.

"One of our granddaughters went on a mission trip to Kenya to share the gospel, and she sent us a picture of her ministering to the people there. In the photograph she was sharing the salvation story using the *Wordless Book* that John has used in his ministry many times. That picture is very special to us, because it reminds us of what is really important and how far God has brought us in our lives together."

The cover of the *Wordless Book* is green, inside there is a gold page that represents Heaven, there is a dark page that represents sin, there is a red page that represents the blood Christ shed for us, and there is a white page that represents how once we accept Jesus into our lives our sins are washed away, and our spirits are as white as snow.

"I know that God had a reason for putting John and I together," says Angie, "and that is to further His kingdom."

37

Hally Yust was born into a sports family. An accomplished athlete by the age of nine years old, basketball and waterskiing were two of her passions. Her father, Shon, says that Hally was probably destined to love basketball, as she was born during the 2005 NCAA Basketball Tournament. When Hally was less than a week old she attended her first official sporting event, when her mother, Jenny Yust, took infant Hally and her older sister Macy to watch their older brother Parker's youth league basketball game, where Hally's father, Shon, coached Parker's team. Later Hally would ask her parents each fall when basketball season began, "When will Daddy be my coach?"

As the years passed it would be a regular occurrence to see Hally dribbling and passing the basketball along the side courts at Parker's games. As Hally grew, so did her love of basketball. Before long she would play on her own youth league basketball teams with her childhood friends, where her father, Shon, coached their teams. In January of 2014, Hally had the opportunity to go to a Harlem Globetrotters game where she got her basketball signed by the Globetrotters.

By May of 2014, Hally, a dedicated and resourceful young lady, had designed for herself a basketball shooting practice chart to record her progress as she consistently worked toward accomplishing her personal goal of making 1000 practice baskets. Hally worked diligently toward her dreams of one day being a part of the Kansas State University Women's

Basketball Team, and playing in the Olympics as a member of the United States Women's Olympic Basketball Team. She would practice faithfully in her driveway every day, rain or shine, night or day. Her dad and brother even made her an official sized half-court basketball court in the barn at the family farm, so she could practice there too when the weather drove her indoors.

Weather permitting, whenever Hally was not playing basketball, she was in the water. Hally loved the water. From the time she was only two years old she attended water ski camps with her sister Macy and brother Parker, where she would participate in shaving cream wars, fishing and frogging events with her family and friends. It wasn't long before Hally would be participating in water ski tournaments. By the age of nine Hally was ranked first in the Midwestern United States for 3-Event Water Skiing.

Sometimes Hally and her family would travel to water ski tournaments in the family RV. It was at these water ski tournaments that Hally helped sell lemonade to raise money for her ski coach who was battling leukemia.

In addition to her passion for sports, Hally shared a strong commitment to faith with her family. Hally began her life on earth in God's house when her mom Jenny's water broke on Sunday, March 13, 2005, at Olathe Christian Church. Early the next morning a beautiful, blond-haired, blue-eyed, fair-skinned baby girl joined her big brother and sister in the Yust family. As a child, Hally loved to hear her mother, Jenny, read to her the Biblical story of Samson. Later when Hally was five years old while attending the baptismal service for her sister Macy, Hally confessed that she too wanted to live her life for Christ. She confirmed her commitment to Jesus by publicly professing her faith when she was baptized, February 26, 2013.

Hally loved going to the local Vacation Bible school, and as was in step with her competitive nature, she strove to finish her AWANA book before everyone else in her AWANA club. Hally also loved shining Christ to the poor and needy, being a part of God's hands and feet by serving at the Center of Grace in Olathe, Kansas, raising money to help send Bibles to Haiti, running in the Kids' Marathon for Team ZAT, and giving money to any charity she could. In her private time, Hally wrote many praise songs to God and spent a part of each night reading her Bible in bed with her big sister, Macy. She passionately memorized her AWANA verses, wrote songs of praise in private to the Lord, and kept a journal of her prayers.

In the summer of 2014, Hally and the rest of the Yust family were busy doing all of their normal family activities; helping out around the family farm, going to water ski practices, traveling to competitions, attending summer camps, swimming in the family pool, keeping playdates with friends, and an annual family trip to the Bahamas.

The weekend of July 4th started out with fireworks and a trip to the lake with grandparents and cousins. Then on Monday morning July 7th, Hally woke up sick. By Tuesday morning, Hally's bewildered parents rushed her to the emergency room, and by that night Hally Nicole Yust was brain dead.

Everyone, including the doctors, couldn't understand what had gone so terribly wrong so quickly. The next day an infectious disease doctor discovered that Hally's brain had been attacked by an amoeba found in lakes and ponds all over the United States. The amoeba causes an infection, primary amoebic meningoencephalitis (PAM), which is 98% fatal. No one will ever understand or know why Hally Yust was taken from earth at such a young age, but all who love her have one prayer: that her story may lead others to trust in Jesus Christ, as Savior.

The Yust's son, Parker, was a few years younger than Nathan. Even though they were not the same age, the boys knew each other from attending birthday parties as kids and Parker also played in some of the same football programs as Nathan. But since Parker was a few years behind Nathan in school the two boys never played on the same team together.

When Nathan passed away Parker attended the Celebration of Life Service for Nathan where the Nathan Project was launched and some of his friends went forward after the service and received study Bibles. Parker says that it was inspiring to see that night how the Stiles family was turning something that was tragic into something good by gifting away the Bibles. "There were a lot of cool things that began happening throughout our community as Ron began giving away the Bibles, and a lot of my friends at that time began reading their Bibles and attending church." There was no way to know at the time Nathan died, that a few years later that Hally would tragically die. And while the family was there together at the hospital with Hally they talked about what things were most important to them, and what they wanted to do to honor Hally. They chose two things. First, they too chose to begin gifting away Bibles. The Bibles they gift are similar to the Bibles gifted through the Nathan Project, but geared more toward younger kids, whereas the Nathan Project's Bibles are more for high schoolers and young adults.

In addition to the Bible Ministry the Yust family also began a scholarship program in Hally's memory supporting the Kansas State University Women's Basketball Team.

"It has been very interesting in our community to see how the Nathan Project Ministry has affected so many people in prisons and young men, women and teenagers, where as Hally's Bibles have gone more toward Vacation Bible schoolers and kids more her own age," Jenny said. "It is amazing to see how God works all things together for His good. We are hoping that in following in the Stiles' footsteps, that our family, as is the case with the Stiles family, is also taking a tragedy and pointing people back to the hope of Christ and having more of an eternal perspective, rather than our life on this earth is all there is."

"Being honest," Shon says, "at first we did not know where we were going to go with this tragedy of losing Hally. At that point we were just trying to hold our family together.

We did not have a plan for how this ministry of giving away Bibles would all work out in the beginning. I know at times Jenny can feel like she is on an island by herself doing all the things involved with coordinating the gifting away of a couple of thousand Bibles a year. But it seems like in the last year God has come around us, and He has given us more energy. He's pushing us even more; we are starting to gift Bibles away outside the country now. We are getting more requests for Bibles all the time; like can we get 100 Bibles here or 50 Bibles there. Logistics are becoming one of our greatest challenges, and those are great challenges to have. Like how do we get Bibles to children in Haiti, and we just sent a large pallet sized container to Haiti.

"With the Team Hally ministry we also get to go places and talk about the ministry mission," Shon proclaims. "Honestly, I never wanted to be the one to get up and go talk about God because I don't ever feel like I am qualified. I felt like instead of me Lord, 'let somebody else go and do that.' I am more comfortable being the person in the background doing something logistically. But there have been times when this ministry has pushed me in front of a camera to talk about God, even though this is the last thing I would have ever wanted to do before. I hope God is looking down and saying, 'Hey you guys are trying, and that's all I expect.'

"I hope that this ministry continues and maybe we have reached that one person, that one kid, that one adult, I don't know, who comes to know Jesus by reading these Bibles." Shon continues, "We appreciate everybody who has come behind us, and given us strength, and given us hope, and I hope that we continue to go in the direction that God wants this ministry to go."

Parker says, it has been a really awesome opportunity for him to see what God has done in the faith life of their family, and in the lives of people that Team Hally and the Nathan Project ministries have impacted through the gifting of the Bibles. "I'm a student at Kansas State University," says Parker, "and to see what God has done through some of the Bibles I have given out, and what God has done through the Bibles my mom has given out has been amazing, not that we are the one's doing it, it's God that does it. All we are trying to do is to get Bibles into the hands of people who would not have them otherwise. It's been an amazing experience to see what God is doing, and we hope God continues to work in this ministry because we know we cannot do any of this without Him."

"One thing that Ron and Connie did for the Nathan Project Bibles, is that they put Nathan's story on the inside covers of each of the Bibles, and then modeling that, we did that with Hally's story too," Jenny acknowledged. "I have noticed that when people see tragedy, and that even our tragedies are interwoven in God's story, people begin to see that rather than God just being for people who are perfect, the reality is that God is there for everyone, for people that are broken and hurting too. So, I think Nathan's story, and us being allowed to know them and to model our ministry after them has been a really encouraging thing, and maybe drawn a lot of people to read their Bibles that wouldn't have done that before, because of the loss of these two young lives."

One of the events that Team Hally has done to raise money to buy Bibles and create awareness for the ministry mission is a fellowship event they call the Dirty Dash.

"Over the years the Dirty Dash has grown into an event where we have an opportunity to bring a bunch of different people from all over the country together," Parker explains. "We have opened it up to the public now, and we use team captains to raise money for Bibles, it is one of our big fundraisers. We have tons of obstacles in this massive warrior dash mud run type of thing. We have done it for five years now. It's been crazy to see what God has done through that. Bringing people in and giving them the opportunity to hear the Gospel, and also participate in a fun type of race. The race is two-and-one-half miles long, and you go through a pond and massive mud pits, and along the way you also climb over hay bales. We have grown the event each year, and we hope to continue to grow it."

Shon says that it's been exciting over the years to see how the Dirty Dash event has grown. "One of the reasons the Dirty Dash came to be, is that we were planning the race as a company event for our employees the year that Hally died, and she was actually helping to prepare for the event. She had learned to drive the mower that year, and she had been helping us by mowing the path where the event was going to be held. After Hally died we ended up postponing it and doing it in October. That is when our employees started asking us if they could help us create this event in support of Team Hally. I think that first Dirty Dash event is where Team Hally was created, because somebody asked, 'can we make up shirts and put Team Hally on them to support the Yust's,' and that's really where the name Team Hally came from. And from there we have grown it into this fundraising event to support the ministry. It's almost like God had it all planned out after she died, that this Dirty Dash event would be created to support Team Hally, and that would help the ministry to raise money for purchasing the Bibles.

"A lot of people ask us how are the Nathan Project and Team Hally connected?" Shon says. "I think that God probably had it all planned out, from the point that I can't quite understand. But we had a winter storm one Sunday several years ago when church got cancelled. We do not go to the same church as the Stiles, but this winter storm was so severe that everybody's church got cancelled because of this winter blizzard. I don't remember exactly the year, but I believe it was two years before Hally passed away. So, we went over to our next-door neighbor's house, Kathy McAnany, who is Connie Stile's sister and Nathan's aunt, and while we were there that day the Stiles showed up. At that point it had probably been two or three years since Nathan passed away, and I was very captivated by what the Stiles were doing.

"I knew the pain that they had gone through, and yet they were turning the tragedy of what had happened into such good stuff. That is when I talked to the Stiles about maybe getting more involved in their ministry, and possibly going to visit the prisons and some of the things that they were doing so faithfully. Little did we know, that a year and a half later we would be going through this same type of tragedy. So, I really think that God was probably planting some seeds even then.

"You know in life, like we learned in our church service recently, we are all headed toward some type of tragedy. Whether we like it or not, there is going to be tribulation in our lives. And it's how you handle that tribulation, how you look toward God in those moments is what matters. So, I think at the point when we were in the hospital, trying to figure out what are we going to do, to first of all keep our family together, and two, to keep us focused toward God, obviously the Bible conversation came up. And I do not know the exact timing of it, but one of us, Jenny or I, we got on the phone and we talked to the Stiles and we said, 'Hey we are thinking about doing this Bible ministry, and we don't want to tread on your ministry. We don't want to feel like we are duplicating efforts.' And Ron just said, 'No, that is not going to happen, you guys should do everything you can. If it is furthering the word of the Lord you should go for it."

Jenny recalls that Shon called Ron after Hally died and asked him to bring the Nathan Bibles to Hally's service. "We did not prepare Bibles right away because her service was in just a few days of her passing," says Jenny. "So, Ron and Connie were actually there in the back of the room at Hally's Celebration of Life Service with the Nathan Project Bibles, and they gave away several hundred Bibles at Hally's service, so God was already planting those seeds right away."

"Soon thereafter we had to make a decision about what Bible we were going to use and where we were going with the ministry," Shon recalls. "It was apparent that Ron's work was focused more on reaching the teenagers, and Hally was quite a bit younger than Nathan when the two passed away, so we decided it would probably be better for us to focus more on the junior level kids in our ministry since that was more in line with Hally's age group. Both of the Bibles are great Bibles for whatever demographic you are trying to reach. In our ministry work we target vacation Bible schoolers which tend to be the younger youth. And we supply Bibles to orphanages which also tends to be the younger kids. It's been amazing how the two ministries have kind of been intertwined.

"I think at one-point Jenny was actually traveling around with some of the Nathan Project Bibles in her car and if the person being given a Bible was older, she would give away the Nathan Project Bible. If they were a younger person, she would give away the Team Hally, *Following Jesus* Bible. It's been interesting and to even cap this off, there is another family in our church who gives away younger children's Bibles in honor of their child. So, it's really been kind of a trifecta of people who have come together in our community who give Bibles away. Maybe in ten years or so we might be able to look back and see how many Bibles have been given away, and to see how people's lives have been changed by receiving a Bible from these ministries, that were begun after these tragedies that have affected these families."

"It's been really cool to see how God has orchestrated having a middle-aged children's Bible, a teenage Bible and then a younger age children's Bible. No one could have planned that out. I think it points back to God, and seeing how He has been working in these ministries through the gifting away of these Bibles to reach people for Christ has been really exciting," exclaims Parker.

Once Team Hally began, the Yust family created a website, *TeamHally.org*. The website says that the goal of Team Hally is, "to magnify the Lord in all that we do. Our mission is to provide Bibles to anyone who wants to read God's Word, including individuals, Sunday schools, Vacation Bible schools, local charities, schools, neighbors, prisoners, hospitals, groups overseas and many others."

There is a section on the site where the family shares their memories of Hally, and their thoughts on the importance of reading the Bible and discussing what we read with others.

Quoting from the Team Hally website, "There are many Bible reading plans available now through a variety of websites and books. Personally, we have enjoyed reading and discussing the Bible in groups with friends. Some of our favorite books to read and discuss with friends have been Luke and Philippians. One of our favorite ways to discuss the Bible with friends is by reading through a specific chapter as a group, and having each person individually share their favorite verse from the chapter and the significance it has to them. This allows a deeper understanding of the Bible and deeper relationships with Christian friends.

"We also feel it is helpful to ask for God to guide us as we read the Bible. A simple prayer is a great idea. You can use the following prayer if you do not have one already:

"God, help me in the reading, hearing, and understanding of your Word, Amen."

38

"Not long after I gave my life to Christ and started walking with Him, I went to see my attorney. When I entered his office, he looked like he had seen a ghost."

"He said, 'What happened to you? You don't look the same.'"

"'I'm not the same,' I replied."

"My attorney could actually see a difference in my physical appearance. I told him I really needed to talk to him about the change in me.

"'We have a problem,' I told him."

"'What's that Bill?' he asked."

"The reason I don't look the same is because I am a Christian now. And God has made some radical changes in me. One is, I can't lie anymore."

"My lawyer put his face in his hands and took a deep breath."

"'You're right Bill. We do have a problem.'"

In Bill Corum's autobiography, *The Ultimate Pardon,* he speaks candidly about his life, the first part of which he lived in the world of drugs, violence and crime. But then, when he was at his lowest point with his life spiraling out of control, and there was seemingly nowhere else to turn for help, Bill gave his life to Christ. From that point forward, the Holy Spirit made a radical change in the life of Bill Corum.

The man who was once on trial for crimes that could have sent him to prison for the rest of his life, would be miraculously pardoned, and then used by God to travel to prisons across the United States and Europe, doing ministry missions work building reservoirs in Africa.

One night after the Lord came into Bill's life and began changing him, his wife Debbie asked Bill to go with her to a Bible study. Over the next several months Bill and Debbie would become very close friends with the couple who was hosting this Bible study.

"We were at their house one night a few months later when they gave me a book that changed my life, *There's Dynamite in Praise*, by Don Gossett. In this book the author explains the power of praise and how praise is a key that unlocks doors nothing else will unlock," Bill says. "Praise is the most mentioned commandment in the Bible for a good reason. Psalm 22:3 says, the Lord 'inhabits' our praise. Inhabits means dwells, stays, lives, etc., so when we praise Him, He comes. If He comes, He wants to stay. How do you get in His presence and stay there? We can achieve that by continually praising Him.

"I have looked for joy in a multitude of ways in my life. I bought eleven brand new cars in thirteen years. I used drugs, drank alcohol, bought jewelry, chased women, but they only brought me temporary joy. I have now found joy unspeakable. Psalm 16:11 says, *'In His presence is fullness of joy.'* I experienced what I thought was joy in a lot of different ways, but never experienced fullness of joy until I was in the presence of the Lord. I have learned that the key to staying in His presence, and therefore having fullness of joy, is to praise Him."

Not long after Bill became a Christian, he went back into the most dangerous and darkest parts of Kansas City, to the same places he had sold and bought drugs, where the drug dealers, addicts and prostitutes roamed the streets. It was there in the streets, that Bill and his wife, Debbie, began their ministry.

"Sometimes we stayed out there for hours just walking, praying and witnessing to whoever would listen," Bill recalls. "I felt like I needed to do something to make up for all the wrong I had done in the streets. I was a brand-new Christian then, and at that time I didn't know that I did not have to earn God's love. His love is unconditional, and when we say 'yes' to Jesus, we don't have to do penance.

"During the time we did street ministry, we also volunteered at the Kansas City Rescue Mission two or three nights a week. We helped serve meals to the homeless and wash dishes. On occasion I got to share my testimony with those who came into the chapel. I will never forget the night a man came through the line, handed me his dirty dishes, and asked me, 'Why do you wash my dirty dishes?'

"I do it because Jesus loves you, and so do I," Bill replied.

"He asked me if he could talk to me later. When we got together, he told me he was a doctor. He had lost his family and began drinking. He became an alcoholic, and over time lost his practice and everything he had. He became homeless and had lived in the streets for years.

"I met with him for several weeks and he finally made a decision to try Jesus and get his life back on track. He then returned home and reconciled with his family. He was a changed man."

Then later in 1988, Bill had been a Christian for five years when someone asked him to go on a prison mission weekend with Bill Glass. Bill Glass had been a professional football player for the Cleveland Browns. Once he retired from professional football, he began preaching in some of Billy Graham's Evangelical crusades. By this time Bill had been speaking at youth meetings and high schools, sharing an anti-drug message whenever he was able.

"I am honored that I have been going into prisons with Bill Glass now for over 33 years. He has truly been a mentor to me in many ways, and I am proud to call Bill Glass my friend. My wife, Debbie, and I were privileged to attend the

40th Anniversary Celebration of his ministry in 2012, where we celebrated over one million incarcerated men and women who have made decisions to follow Christ."

Later in January of 1992, as an answer to prayer, Bill and his wife started Prison Power Ministries, Inc.

"From the beginning God opened doors all over the place for us," says Bill. "One of the first doors the Lord opened was at Municipal Correctional Institution in Kansas City, Missouri's city jail. I heard they didn't have a chaplain so I went to apply for the job. I will never forget the day I met Mr. Burt and Bill Howard. Mr. Burt was the superintendent and Bill Howard was a captain who had been there for many years. Mr. Burt told me they had known for a long time there was a chaplain coming – they just didn't know what he would look like.

"I became the full-time chaplain. I received no pay from the city, but God supplied all of our needs. Debbie and I decided when we started Prison Power Ministries, that we didn't want to ask anyone for money. Professionals told me we would never make it unless we followed the fundraising models. God took care of us the entire time we ran the ministry; we were never late on a bill, and never missed a payment."

In 1995, Bill was asked to go to Germany to share his testimony. He and his wife, Debbie, flew to Frankfurt, Germany, then from Frankfurt Bill began a series of speaking engagements in churches, prisons and was interviewed on radio and television where Bill shared his salvation story. Their initial agenda included nearly forty meetings spread out over a period of 27 days. Once the tour began and Bill began to share his story, there was such a demand for him to speak and share the Gospel message, that his itinerary grew from 40 meetings to 65, all done within the original 27-day time period.

"We ministered in prisons, jails, schools, churches, coffee houses, and on television and radio stations. I spoke in a prison in former East Germany where no American had ever been.

They allowed me to share my story and preach to the entire staff and new officers in training. It was most likely the first time some of them had heard the Gospel, and the Spirit of the Lord really moved.

"I was told when we arrived in Germany, I should not give alter calls, because German men were very reserved and would not respond. There was never a time when I did not feel I was supposed to give men the chance to give their hearts to Jesus. The men who advised me not to give altar calls were amazed. I told them it was not me; it was the Holy Spirit drawing them."

Bill says today that he feels like the richest man on Earth because God has taken him to a place of peace that he never dreamed possible. He is thankful for the blessings God has bestowed on him as He has transformed Bill's life. God has given him things that no amount of money could buy.

"God gave me my mind back. In 1983, I couldn't have carried on a conversation with someone, because in the middle of a sentence I would forget what I was saying. I did so many drugs and drank so much alcohol, my mind was fried. God renewed my mind, and made it better than it was before I ever used drugs or alcohol.

"God gave me my wife back. God healed our marriage and gave her grace to put up with me. She was able to forgive me. How much would you pay to get your wife back?

"God gave me my sons and daughters back. Through years of prayer, and sitting down with them one-on-one and repenting to them, our relationship has been restored. How much would you give to get your kids back?"

Bill says that over these past thirty years he has enjoyed peace that he never would have experienced before giving his life to Christ. He has learned that the peace that passes all understanding, the type of peace that Paul speaks about in Philippians 4:7, has come from his personal relationship with Christ and the time he has spent reading his Bible and studying God's Word.

"Jesus saved me, but His Word is what changed me," declares Bill. "Eternity is forever, and this life is just a vapor. It seems that the entire world wants to chase the things that mean the least, the money, the material things, the power, the titles. In the end, we will face God alone; we will take nothing else with us. Everything else will be left behind."

Bill says he has never been the type of person to live a boring lifestyle. His life before Christ, was by all accounts a wild ride. In his autobiography, *The Ultimate Pardon*, Bill tells the story of a day when he was about to take the stage at a ministry service in a federal prison, and one of the inmates approached Bill with his concerns about what his life would be like if he decided to become a Christian.

This young man said to Bill, "I am thirty-two years old; I've been in and out of the prison system since I was twelve. For twenty years, I've either been locked up, on parole or probation. I'd like to be a Christian, but I'm afraid it will be too boring."

"I told him if you're talking about taking your Bible to church on Sunday, then going home and putting it back on the shelf till next Sunday, it's boring.   But, if you're talking about living for Jesus 24/7, there's nothing boring about it," exclaims Bill. "I'm not a man who can live a boring life. Let me tell you a little about my life before I was a Christian.

"My partner, Kenny, he had a Turbo Carrera Porsche that would go 185 mph. We used to get in it and go 150 mph on I-70 through downtown Kansas City. If you think going three times the speed limit with an Uzi laying in the backseat is boring, you should go with me.

"I used to go into a shooting gallery; and I'm not talking about a place to target practice, I'm talking about a place you go to shoot dope. I would walk in and lay my .357 Magnum on one side of me and my .9mm on the other. I'd open a box with six or eight ounces of cocaine and ten thousand dollars or more in it, just hoping someone would try and take my cocaine or my money so I could shoot them. If you think that's boring, you should go to a shooting gallery with me. Remember, I said I can't live a boring life.

"Now, as a Christian, let me tell you what I do. I go to death row and sit on a concrete floor. I hold a man's hand through the bars of a six-by-nine-foot cell he's been locked in for seventeen years, and pray with him to receive Christ. If you think that's boring, come go with me to death row.

"I go to San Quentin prison, where there are six thousand inmates. More than half of them never get a letter or a visit. When you're in prison for fifteen or twenty years and you never have a letter or a visit, you get pretty angry. They let one thousand men at a time out on the big yard. I go down to the iron pile and lift weights with some of the angriest men in the world. If you think that's boring, come go with me to San Quentin.

"I go to the AIDS wards where men are dying, they can barely whisper, they are so weak. They will ask, 'Please pray for me.' Sometimes I get to lead them to Christ before they die. If you think that's boring, come go with me to the AIDS wards.

"I then shook the young man's hand and walked up the steps of the platform to speak. The Lord told me to tell that whole story again to the rest of the men in the assembly that day. When I gave the alter call, that young man was one of the first ones to come forward. Praise the Lord."

✳ ✳ ✳

"Along with the ministry service that day, Bill had organized a car and motorcycle show for the inmates," Ron recalls. "When we arrived outside the wall, the vehicles were already there inside. Before long the inmates started to show up. They were allowed to look at the cars and motorcycles, and then they moved on into the cafeteria where the volunteers helping with the service served them hamburgers and hot dogs.

"As I was walking around the prison yard that day waiting for the service to begin, I was thinking that I had been doing ministry in the detention centers long enough now that I should see some of the young men I have worked with in the past in here today. It was not long before two of the young men I knew from the detention center ministry recognized me, and they came over to speak with me. We stood there for a while talking about the changes in their lives since we had last seen each other and some of their past problems that took them down the road to incarceration. Drug abuse is a common denominator in so many of these inmates' pasts, and for these two young men drugs was a large part of the reason they were behind bars.

"One of them told me that he had a young child now, and he smiled as he spoke of her. Later the three of us sat down together and talked about their lives in prison and some potential game plans to help make their lives better once they have served their time and are released.

"Both of them told me they still have the Bibles they were given in the juvenile system, and as we talked, I stressed to them the importance of daily reading and studying God's Word, and how that can change lives. The service was scheduled to begin at 6 p.m., so I asked them if they were going and they said they were. I told them I would see them there.

"I waited for them as the hour drew close and then along came one of them," Ron says. "He said his friend wanted to come too but he was concerned that he might not be able to go since he had not signed up to attend the service ahead of time. I told them I thought we could work that out. It was not long before both of them were admitted into the auditorium and were sitting to my left. This was to be a two-hour service, and it began with some wonderful music performed by ministry volunteers who themselves were prior inmates. These men were back inside the prison trying to help the current inmate population find Jesus, the same way these men had found Jesus while they were inmates.

"It was extremely hot in the facility this day in late August. There was no air conditioning in this building, just a few fans blowing hot air across the crowded room. But even so, there was not one complaint from the inmates. They all made the point of thanking the volunteers for coming and sharing the gospel with them.

"Soon Bill Corum took the microphone and he announced the names of the three speakers who would be addressing the group. The first speaker was sitting in front of me, and as I was sharing something I had read in the book of John with my two young friends sitting to my left, he turned and said that they had just discussed those passages the night before in a Bible study he was attending. This man had also spent time in prison, and while he was incarcerated, he met Bill Corum. He said Bill was the person who helped lead him to Jesus.

"When this gentleman took the stage to speak, Bill told the crowd that this man had once been an inmate in this same prison, but had given his life to Christ and now had become Bill's pastor. As this former inmate shared his testimony, you could see and feel the impact his message was having on the men. Once he finished speaking, the next speaker addressed the men and then the next. When the last speaker finished his presentation, he offered an invitation for anyone who wanted to give their life to Christ to come forward and receive Jesus.

"My two young friends sitting next to me, both threw their hands in the air and went forward. I immediately stood and walked up between them; I placed my arms across their shoulders as we stood their side by side together. They were both in tears, and one said to me, 'This is real I can feel it,' and I said, 'yes, it is.' As we were standing there, one of them looked down toward my feet and saw that one of my shoelaces was untied, he then bent down and tied my shoe. 'He was taking care of the old man,' I thought. In that moment his bending down to help me meant a lot to me. Then, as I stood there next to these two men, they gave their lives to Christ.

"Later, as the evening came to an end, I was speaking with Bill's pastor and he talked about his desire to help youth in the inner city. I asked him if they needed some Bibles for their youth ministry? He told me they were in need of Bibles, but they had found working with the youth that they could not use the King James version, because the kids had trouble understanding the way the text was written in those Bibles. I handed him a New Life Translation Study Bible and told him they were student versions written for teens, and that we give those away through the Nathan Project. He told me that he had been praying for study Bibles, and he could use at least 20 more as soon as we could get them to him if we had any more. I told him I had 48 study Bibles in my truck, and asked, 'Would tonight be soon enough?'

"It was a perfect end to the evening."

39

"Why did God create rainbows?"

Nick Sprague is a college student who plays on the offensive line for the MidAmerica Nazarene University football team. Nick says there was a day not too long ago at football practice when he and the other offensive linemen had just finished some grueling practice drills, and they were all really tired so they took a break to get some water. It had been raining at practice earlier that day, and after Nick had gotten some water he turned around and looked up into the sky where he saw this huge, beautiful rainbow. It was the biggest, fullest rainbow Nick had ever seen.

Once Nick saw the rainbow, he felt an overwhelming urge to ask the other guys with him at practice that day if they knew the purpose of the rainbow, and what was the origin and significance of the rainbow in scripture? Nick says it was a bit out of character for him to ask a question like that during a football practice.

"Looking back on it now it was kind of funny because I normally don't talk a lot during football practice because I am in a get it done mode." Nick continues, "So I asked everyone this question about the rainbow and no one knew the answer. They were throwing out things like it has a pot of gold at the end of it, or it leads to San Francisco, which was kind of funny because it ran north and south and not towards San Francisco at all. Afterwards, I told the guys that the rainbow was a visible sign that God would never flood the Earth again. It signified the promise made by God to all people after He chose Noah to build an arc and survive the great flood, that God would never flood the Earth again, as He began through Noah and his family to repopulate the Earth. It was a really cool and small moment, something that happens more and more now that I am becoming more in tune with things that continue to happen with the group of guys."

For Nick Sprague the idea of sharing the Gospel is nothing new. Nick remembers that he felt a call on his life to enter into the ministry while he was a middle school student. Over the years that initial call has become clearer. He is now attending MidAmerica Nazarene University with intentions of attending seminary after graduation.

"When I was in the eighth grade, I received my call to go into the ministry. When I talk about my call from God, I mean that it was very clear to me, that He wanted me to go into ministry and to spread His Word. Over the years, this calling has continued to grow and develop, and be confirmed by people I trust and value. God has developed this calling into a place that my heart breaks for the family atmosphere here in America. I think the American view of families is broken, and it isn't going to be fixed anytime soon. I come from a divorced family, and it breaks my heart that the divorce rate in America is at 50%. I feel that God has called me to help families; meaning kids, teens, young adults, and their parents as well. I want to show people how to have a Christ-filled life and home. So, with all of that being said, I see myself becoming either a youth pastor, family pastor or a lead pastor, with the previous being my point of focus."

Before attending MNU on a combination of athletic and academic scholarships, Nick was a student at Spring Hill High School, where he played on the football team. Nick remembers hearing about Nathan's story as he was growing up, and that there was a memorial placed in the Spring Hill locker room in memory of Nathan. Nick says he met Ron Stiles when he was in the eighth grade, and was familiar with the Nathan Project

Ministry mission of giving away New Living Translation Study Bibles.

It was a few years later, while Nick was a freshman at MidAmerica Nazarene University, that an unexpected email came his way, which gave him an opportunity to serve in a youth ministry capacity in a low-income area church.

"I had just started school at MNU, and I was reading a book titled, *Do Hard Things*. The premise of the book was that teenagers needed to stop making excuses, and that if they do, they can do great things. As I was reading this book, I got an email about a church that needed a youth pastor. I thought initially that I would leave that to the older people, but instead, I looked down at my book and thought to myself, that I needed to practice what I was reading. So, I emailed the church back and applied for the position. Long story short, I have spent two years with them in their time of transition."

In the church where Nick started working as a youth pastor, many of the kids in their youth program did not have their own Bibles. It was then that Nick thought about the Nathan Project. He contacted Ron about getting some Bibles from the Nathan Project, and Ron gave Nick enough study Bibles to provide one for every young person in his church's youth group.

"At my church, I implemented the use of the Bibles almost immediately and the reactions to them are so different it is amazing. Some of the kids took to them and started using them as their main Bible right away, while others preferred to still use their own Bibles. But the reaction that is most noticeable, is that the kids always take them to give to their friends who they are witnessing to. It has been wonderful to see the kids taking and giving away these Bibles. I know those Bibles and the kids in our youth group are making a difference in our community."

Nick says he loves to see the kids in his youth group ministry bring the Bibles with them to Bible study and see where the Bibles have been dog-eared and highlighted, and often filled with post it notes marking the passages the kids are studying. "I can see the kids are reading and studying these Bibles," exclaims Nick.

"One of the beautiful things about working with teenagers is that they are in such a point of transition in their lives. This point of transition is a beautiful launching point, which if guided through correctly can put a teenager in a great place as they head into adulthood."

Nick believes the youth pastor's role is to help support the parents/family to aid the student through what can be a confusing time in their lives. Nick says this transitional period is also the thing that most people get mixed up about when they are working with teenagers.

"Teens are going through changes in every aspect of their development," Nick continues, "the most obvious of which is their physical transition we know as puberty. But most people don't realize that they are also going through a psychosocial change, cognitive changes and identity changes, and teens are going through a faith development change as well. If we ignore any of these as youth ministers, then we are putting the kids we are ministering to in danger of being left behind.

"In the youth ministry, it is also important to provide ways for the kids to practice what you are teaching them. So, if you are teaching about service then provide ways for them to serve. If you are teaching about witnessing and telling them what you believe then you have to provide ways for them to witness. Having the Bibles provided by the Nathan Project has created an easy bridge for the students to study their Bibles and serve in our community, by gifting away the Bibles to people they are now ministering to."

In addition to his work in his youth ministry position, Nick also began to feel that God was calling him to minister to the other players on his football team, so he started a Bible study with the guys on his college football team as well.

"I started the Bible study with my football team because there were so many guys who had no idea about who God was, and they needed to hear the Gospel."

When Nick decided to begin the Bible study with his football team, he again called on the Nathan Project for New Living Translation Study Bibles, and once again Ron donated Bibles to support Nick in his Bible study ministry.

"I get Bibles from Ron about twice a year now, and I have given away over two hundred Bibles in my two years of ministry. One to every kid in my youth group, and one to every guy on the football team, there were even Bibles given to some of the players on the MNU women's softball team as well.

"When I was making my decision about where to attend college, I chose MNU because it was the local school in our area, and the school that was always talked about in our church and youth group. I had always dreamed of playing college football and MNU seemed liked the best option for me. I also chose MNU because of their ministry program. I am on scholarship for both academics and football here at MNU."

Since Nick has been at MNU, the opportunity to work as a youth pastor and the experience of leading the Bible study with his teammates on the football team has further solidified Nick's decision to go into the ministry once he graduates.

"The combination of both of these ministries has given me a better understanding of servant leadership. By walking the walk of faith with our youth group and leading the Bible study, I have gained valuable experience that will help me to lead my congregation when I graduate from seminary. Once I become a pastor, I hope to give my congregation authentic leadership through my actions and provide ways for them to practice what I preach. Both of these ministry experiences have been great for my future career as a pastor and the Bibles gifted to me by the Nathan Project have been an important asset for everyone involved in these ministries."

Nick believes that student athletes on a high school or college campus are in a unique position to use their platform given to them by their athletic gifts as a way to reach their classmates for Christ. Helping student athletes realize the power of their athletic platform is something he is stressing to the other athletes on campus who are attending his Bible study.

"All athletes everywhere, whether they like it or not have a platform to speak up for Christ, and their peers respect it when they do. But that being said, as an athlete, you have to give the respect right back to your other peers, without this mutual respect you have no platform. As an athlete there are many ways you can use your God given voice, but I chose to use mine by purposely praying before games where others could see me with the rest of my team in the middle of the field. In college I pray with my teammates in the end zone before the game. I also follow my actions with my words, because if I didn't then my actions mean nothing.

"To be an effective leader for Christ, your actions and words must be thorough throughout your every being. We cannot be the hypocrites that sometimes people of faith are known for. This attitude of servant leadership is developed over time. It comes with time, practice and patience. You also have to be honest with others around you and tell them when you have messed up. There is no pressure here except for bettering your own relationship with God, and once you have done that, your actions with others will be a byproduct of this deepening of faith."

The Bibles donated through the Nathan Project, as was the case with his youth ministry, have been an integral part of Nick's campus ministry.

"Several individuals responded by telling me how participating in the Bible study had deepened their understanding of the "basics" of Christianity, and that they were happy that they had participated in the Bible study.

"Another individual who was a part of our campus Bible study responded this way, 'I have always had faith in who God is and that's because of my family. I have never trusted organized religion, until this Bible study where I realized how important the fellowship of organized religion is.'"

Nick says a big part of the Bible study's impact on the student athletes was the easy to read and understand text and study notes of the New Living Translation Bibles.

"The New Living Translation made it possible to put the scriptures in a more readable and understandable form for most of the people in the group. One person said, 'I love this translation! I have only ever used the King James version and that was so hard and difficult to understand it was ridiculous. I actually enjoy reading the Bible now.'

"The guys responded pretty positively too about the opportunity to learn and talk with other people of like mind, (football players/athletes) and be able to explore the basics of Christianity without the judgment.

"This is my second time leading this Bible study and it has been an amazing experience, trying my hand at using sports ministry to reach student athletes. I have learned tools and ways of communicating with my peers that resonate with them. I have learned just how important it is to come from underneath them while teaching and not from above. Because even a little bit of a tone hinting towards being condescending and they would shut down.

"When I was working in a very low-income church, the Nathan Project provided us with Bibles that we could give away to the kids when they wouldn't normally be able to buy themselves study Bibles. One thing I see that is an immediate need for the Nathan Project is for there to be more people who are aware of their ministry mission so that more people would help fund their ministry so that they can keep giving away these amazing Bibles to those in need.

"I have seen these Bibles gifted to us used on many levels. We have handed the Bibles out at community events and I've seen people come back to our church because of the Bibles. I have also seen teens walk into my office with passages highlighted, notated, sticky notes all over the place and the

Bibles were falling apart. This has been such a blessing to those that they touch, these Bibles are being used for the Glory of God, and I hope they are continued to be used in this fashion.

"Campus and sports ministry are very different from what you experience within the church. When you are leading either of these ministries you come in contact with more people that would never step in a church. These people are wonderful people but have usually been hurt from the church, so they wouldn't come back to one. This gives you a wonderful opportunity to minister to and change their perceptions of what church is.

"I have loved leading these ministries, and I hope I can continue to be involved in sports ministry all the way through my pastoral career."

Nathan and Natalie
at a wedding

Nathan and Natalie on Nerd Day at school

Natalie and her husband, Drew, at their wedding with her grandparents,
Judy and Eldon Morrison

Drew, Josie, and Natalie with Christine Musisi and Deo Musisi from
Uganda at Natalie and Drew's wedding

Ron's children - Natalie, Josie, Nick, Clinton, and Nathan (clockwise left to right)

Ron's parents, Robert and Catherine Stiles

Nathan and Cole Broockerd

Cole and Amy Broockerd on their wedding day

A seat reserved in memory
of Nathan at Mike Reynolds'
wedding

Natalie, Mike Reynolds and Connie at Mike's wedding

Nathan and Ron at the father-son softball game

Jose Vega and Tom Carbajo at the 2020 AFC Championship Game

Connie, Andrew Hudson, Peyton Hudson, Natalie, Ron and Josie
at Andrew and Peyton's wedding

Nathan Project Study Bibles in the Philippians

Students at Kansas College in Uganda receive Bibles from The Nathan Project in August of 2012. Photo by Brent Messimer.

Nathan, Connie and Natalie the summer of 2010

40

Uganda N.O.W.
Written By
Josie Stiles

I was sitting in church and the yearly brochure for mission trips had been passed out. I opened the brochure and read the location and purpose for each trip. The primary goals were to pour concrete and build houses (I couldn't bench press the bar without weights on it in high school) and to visit orphanages. I pictured myself surrounded by lots of children and thought, "Not for me." I glanced through them quickly; I had prayed that if I could legitimately help, I would consider a mission trip. After all, it makes no sense to go on a trip when you have nothing to offer. My eyes flashed over a trip to train teachers in Uganda. My eyes froze and my heart stopped. I am a teacher who sat through teacher trainings and helped lead trainings in my high school.

My heart rate increased. My tidy reason not to go on a trip had just been demolished. I began to pray silently, Lord, that is the most expensive trip they are going on this year. If you want me to go, I need you to help me with the funds. I can't afford that.

I sat through the rest of the sermon uncomfortably, not hearing much of what was said, but, instead, thinking about all the reasons why I should not go to Africa. After the sermon was over, I saw a friend's mother walk toward me. For years she and her husband had been having a lot of us over every Sunday after church for dinner. She loves others so naturally and I adore her walk with Jesus. She looked me in the eyes, "Josie, I saw the trip to Uganda and thought about you, and that you need to go. I can't pay for it all, but I will give you $800 toward it."

I was dumbfounded, "Okay Lord, I will go to the informational meeting and find out more about it."

Driving down the road I felt as if I had just jumped into hyperspace (bear with me, Bubby/Nathan loved Star Wars), except the blur around me was not from the light of stars, but of white from a massive snowstorm. Lord, the weather is horrible; I bet this meeting is cancelled. I wanted to turn around but knew I would forever regret it. I pulled into the parking lot of "The Barn" at church and paused. The Barn had been refurbished: concrete floors, carpet, couches, round tables encircled with chairs, smells from the coffee bar diffuse through the air, a small stage up front with a warm glow from the lights above, and a sound booth upstairs looking over it all. I had spent many hours in it helping out with the young adult ministry. It was a familiar place, a comfortable place. I have always liked comfortable.

As I walked into The Barn, I saw a group of smiling faces, bright photographs that looked like they could have been in a National Geographic article, and African artifacts dispersed on tables all around me. I quickly discovered the other three people in the room were leading the trip and I was the only interested newcomer. I released a sigh in my head; I had really wanted to sit in the back and leave shortly after the meeting. As we each exchanged greetings someone asked what I did for a living. Not more than one second after I said, "I teach high school biology," a woman shorter than myself walked up to me and looked intently into my eyes. Her short blondish-gray hair framed her face, and her blue eyes were kind and rimmed with glasses. Her face displayed excitement and tears began to stream past her cheeks as she embraced me exclaiming, "I have been praying for you! You are an answer to my prayers!"

Looks like I'm going to Uganda.

We sat at a round table with wooden mahogany giraffes and pictures of beautiful landscape scattered with palm trees high above a lake for hours, and I listened to their stories. The primary school that we were to visit is in a town called Busagazi. Children in Uganda do not always finish primary school let alone have the opportunity to attend a secondary school because of the cost and pressures to help around the home. Being in such a remote place, Busagazi was no exception to this. Our soon-to-be host in Uganda, Deo Musisi, grew up in Busagazi. He worked hard and performed well in school, resulting in a scholarship that allowed him to complete his education through the university level. Deo speaks many languages and owns a company called DataGrid Africa Center that uses GPS technology to survey land and help monitor natural resources. He is a professor at a university in Kampala, a preacher, has a family of his own, and he and his wife, Christine, are known as "Big Daddy" and "Big Mum" to the students at the pre-school and secondary school they have started. Deo loves the Lord and he and Christine sacrifice a lot to help the people where he grew up to have skills to better support themselves. They built a secondary school in a nearby town called Makindu, so students would have greater access to continue their education. I would not realize this at the time, but as my involvement with missions increased, I would value the Ugandan grassroots movement that we were walking alongside to help however we could.

The American-side of the organization, I was quickly learning, was started by a woman in her early twenties who thought she was going over to do research on primates (the biology teacher in me was thrilled to hear this). As she researched Uganda, her heart began to feel for those she had not met yet. She decided she was going to Uganda and wanted to help those in poverty. She invited her aunt, a doctor who researched tropical diseases and had previous missions experience, Dr. Gail Walter, to go with her. A call went out at a pastors' conference in Uganda that two women from America were coming and wanted to learn about their culture and support them in some way. Deo responded to that call, ended up welcoming two complete strangers into his home, rearranged his schedule (which is not an easy feat), and showed them various places in Uganda, including the schools and different orphanages. They prayed and separately came to the conclusion they were to help with the schools in Busagazi and Makindu. Uganda N.O.W., standing for nutrition, educational outreach, and water, had just been born.

I heard story after story of students who were vulnerable due to the loss of their parents or extreme poverty; these students lived in the dorms in the secondary school (boarding schools are common in Uganda). One goal was to start a child sponsorship program to help them care for more children without diverting resources away from the school. A latrine, that we all lovingly referred to as the squatty potty, a borehole (a clean water source), and classrooms had been recently built at the secondary school. This secondary school was named Kansas College in their appreciation for the building which had been funded by a church in Kansas. In Uganda they use the word "college" for secondary schools and "university" for post-high school education.

Carol, the woman who prayed for me and is generous with hugs, has an elementary education degree and prayed for a high school teacher to join the trip to help her with the teacher training – specifically with the training of the secondary teachers in Makindu. She explained that the teacher training would be nothing more than presenting the type of material I had learned at my professional development trainings. During our first week in Uganda, Carol and I would be training teachers while others on the team were having a Vacation Bible school (VBS), with about 400 elementary-aged children at the Busagazi elementary school. The following week, we would plan to complete a teacher training at the Makindu secondary school, Kansas College. During our time at the schools, the Ugandan and American pastors conducted a conference in Makindu. The ten days in Uganda were going to be busy.

I had walked out of that meeting in The Barn with excitement and fear. I had NEVER considered I would go to Africa, not once. At this point I had been teaching seven years and had some experience with professional development (aka teacher training) and knew it should not be out of my comfort zone, but it was. I also knew that I was out of reasons I could not go to Uganda. I cleared off my snow-covered SUV and headed home, not giving the snowstorm much of a thought at all.

"Yesu Yeebazibwe!"

"Amiina!"

I had been on Ugandan soil less than 24 hours and was already having a lesson in Luganda. When a Ugandan Christian exclaims, "Praise Jesus!" in Lugandan, we were to answer with "Amiina!" which means Amen.

Traveling to Uganda required three flights and 33 hours of travel time. During all of this travel, I was experiencing such a gamut of emotions that sleep eluded me with the exception of a few short naps.

By the time we landed at our final destination, the exhaustion was overshadowed by adrenaline as we were welcomed by our new friends. Deo, Christine (who hugged me so hard she lifted me up and we stayed just that way for more than a few heartbeats), some of their relatives, and friends who had come to the airport to greet us. Though I had not given much thought as what to expect at the airport, it definitely was not this fanfare. There was such joy and excitement through our haze of fatigue.

Once we arrived at Deo and Christine Musisi's suburban home in Entebbe, we were greeted by even more family and friends as well as a spread of Ugandan food. They made us feel welcomed; hospitality and community do not run short in Uganda. I was already learning from our hosts.

After spending a few days in Deo and Christine's home learning information about their culture and a few words in Lugandan, we headed north through a city of over one million, to the secondary school. As we arrived at Kansas College, we met uniformed students with navy slacks or skirts and bright yellow button up shirts.

In the morning, we left Makindu for the primary school is Busagazi. While there, Carol and I had an in-service with the teachers, many of whom worked for little or no pay. Below the brick, open-windowed classroom perched on a hill, hundreds of students had Vacation Bible school with other members of our team. I could hear laughter and cheering while the cool breeze blew through the building.

My nights at Kansas College included hearing Ugandan and American pastor's preaching as part of the conference, the cadence of drums, and the lull of the Ugandans singing late into the night only to be started again hours later. Bats chirped in our rafters (whose presence I appreciated because they kept the mosquito population low). I learned that Bibles in Uganda cost around $50 and are hard to come by. Without being able to read the Word for themselves, these people wanting to learn about God must depend on the interpretation of someone else. Adding insult to injury, there are also churches that persuade the congregation to give money so the pastor can live richly, purchasing an item that will bring you blessings, or purchasing prayers. This is not unlike America, but the difference is that Ugandan believers often do not have the same access to God's Word.

I returned home in early August of 2010, just a few months before Nathan would die from a traumatic brain injury. I taught biology and was an assistant cross-country coach, and Nathan was in his senior year taking upper-level classes and playing football. We were both beyond busy and I couldn't remember the last time that we'd seen each other. The night Nathan was crowned homecoming king, I was there and messaged him later,

"You were always a king in my book Bubby. 😊 Congratulations! Love you!!" In true Nathan fashion he messaged back after the game.

"Ha-ha, thank you sis. 😊 Sorry I couldn't give you and the boys more to cheer about!"

I treasured that I got to say I loved him the last time we communicated, but for a time, could not remember the last time we had spoken in person and I had been given a Nathan hug, the best hug ever. Not being able to remember hurt.

In the spring of 2012, Deo and Christine came over from Uganda with their youngest daughter, Elizabeth, who was months away from turning one. At this point, it had been almost four years since the Uganda N.O.W. founders made their initial visit to Uganda, and there had been many affiliated American visitors on Ugandan soil. They had come to visit churches and individuals that supported the schools.

When Deo and Christine enter a room, it seldom remains unchanged. Christine's memory of details about all of my family and friends is razor sharp. When Christine visited, she remembered all of the family and friends I had mentioned, and to this day will send an occasional message asking about one of them. Their culture values community in such a way that they do not only want to know about how you are doing, but also about how well your community is. In the Ugandan way of thinking, the well-being of your people indicates your well-being. Many Americans are used to single-family housing and being mostly self-reliant. We have our own cars, rooms, and sometimes live alone. I can't help but think that part of the reason people love to be around Deo and Christine is the way in which they genuinely care about the different facets of each person's life.

Deo's personality exudes joy and there is always billowing laughter surrounding him. He is intense, wearing lenses that direct him toward his life's priorities: seeking God's Will, looking after his family, furthering DataGrid, and helping the many students in Busagazi and Makindu to work toward their own ambitions. The air around Deo is never stale, I never bore of conversation with him.

After Deo and Christine visited my dad and step-mom, Connie's, church, my dad invited Dr. Gail, Deo, and Christine over for dinner. Dad and Deo got to talking (zero surprise there, they have a lot in common) and before I knew it, hundreds of Bibles were going to be shipped to Uganda through the Nathan Project. I was planning on going to Uganda a few weeks after Deo and Christine left the U.S., and hoped the Bibles would arrive before me so that I could help hand them out to the secondary students at Kansas College.

When our team arrived in Uganda, the Bibles were in customs with seemingly no one in a hurry to release them. This trip looked different for me as I was able to help with the VBS in Busagazi. This woman, who sat in church just a few years earlier, not wanting to go to Uganda or interact with elementary-aged children there, was now running around in the red dirt playing with them and loving every second.

During my time at Kansas College, I spent time with the students and learned their stories. One girl had been taken away from a witch doctor who had planned to kill her in ritual sacrifice, an act typically performed to bring fortune and good luck. Another came from a tribe that performed female genital mutilation. Interacting with the other students and adults on campus, she was learning that it was not a normal practice everywhere. Another boy had gone home while Deo and Christine were in the U.S., and his mom had been approached by an individual making big promises for her son's success if he switched to a new school. She relented, letting the boy go, but it was discovered that her son, a former Kansas College student, had been a victim of human trafficking. Deo prodded the police to follow the leads he had gathered, and weeks after we left, he was found and able to return to Kansas College.

The problems of these students were so large for their young age. Yet their smiles, laughter, and warmth were larger. I learned human resilience more than I had known was possible and that a loving community pushes out fear and loneliness unlike no other love humans can muster.

-----The intersection of hearts' desires.

As we took our last trip to Busagazi via boda boda we were passing the usual children giggling and shouting, "Bazungu! Bazungu!" (this translates to, "White people! White people!"), dodging random chickens and people along the road. As I was looking at the curve of the rusty colored road in front of me, I had a memory come to life. Nathan was standing in the doorway between the kitchen and dining room of our grandma and grandpa's house. It was August of 2010 before school began. I was telling my family about my first trip to Uganda. As I was finishing, I mentioned that it was hard for Ugandans to access Bibles. Nathan and I were left in the room, and he was stirred that they could not read the Bible for themselves, having instead to rely on others to share and interpret it. He was leaning on the doorway trying to figure out how we could get them their own Bibles. As I heard laughter from the children, the vision of Nathan faded and I saw them running after the boda boda, arms waving and all of the beautiful villagers going about their day.

Tears began to fall, God - You are SO. GOOD.

Nathan's Celebration of Life was held in the gym of the high school one week after he collapsed on the field. On the way to the Celebration, I was exhausted and prayed for God to give me hope. I opened my Bible to Hebrews 11, where it speaks of all the amazing things that happened to those with great faith: Sarah, Abraham, Moses, David…but what about those with great faith who were tortured, flogged, and murdered? What about those for whom it did not end well? The next verses revealed that God had answered my prayer and He met me exactly where I was:

These were all commended for their faith, yet none of them received what had been promised, since God had planned something better for us so that only together with us would they be made perfect.
Hebrews 11:39-40 NIV

One month after the team and I left Uganda, another team arrived. The 500 Bibles were released from customs and handed out among the laughter and bustle of the students at Kansas College.

Nathan's love of the Lord and faithfulness were lived out in how he valued others and in how he spent time in God's Word, even when the days were busy from early morning into late night. Many Ugandan kids will have the same opportunity that Nathan had: to have their very own Bible, and to get to read the story of Jesus for themselves. God was fulfilling the desires of Nathan's heart for God through others, even after his death.

As I left Busagazi, I looked up on the hill at the old, brick walled school building that I had been in years before. This year, Deo had surprised us, by showing us a new school building that was built at the bottom of the hill. It was larger and made of better materials than that old building on the hill, whose stairs and bricks had crumbled. Yet, that old, brick walled school building sat on top of the hill proudly, and overlooked the beautiful children and the beautiful landscape, scattered with palm trees below. Deo's dream of providing for Busagazi's children was now intersecting with my brother's dream.

God – You are SO. GOOD.

41

"I met Ron a couple of years ago when I was in the youth juvenile detention center," the young man said. "It was a Friday night when Ron and Doug showed up for Bible study, that was the first time I met him. Ron gave me a Bible and then once me and the other kids took our seats that first night, we read the chapter in Proverbs for that day of the month and discussed what we had read."

As the young man continued to tell his story, he reflected back on what those Friday night Bible studies meant to him. "Ron's work coming to the detention center and visiting with us pulled me out of a lifestyle that was taking me to a desperate place. Even after I left there and moved on to another facility, he continued to correspond with me through letters. Then, while I was away, he reached out to my mom and sister and helped them too."

For someone who has never visited a detention center, where young people are battling the storms that come into a troubled person's life, as they are struggling to survive, it is hard to understand the realities of what many of these young people are facing. No young person wants to find themselves in this place. But life is fragile, and none of us are above the trials that may take us to a place where things spin sideways. When we find ourselves in those dark places of life, whether we are young or old, rich or poor, regardless of the color of our skin, that is when we are in the greatest need of love and compassion. That is when we need people to come forward and share with us the Good News, that God loves us no matter what. Sharing the gift of a Bible, and spending time with these young people in need is the essence of the Gospel at work in the world. For these young people, many of whom are meeting Christ for the first time, having a Bible that they can read with study footnotes placed strategically throughout, like the Nathan Project New Living Translation Study Bibles, helps these young people to see themselves in the Biblical passages. By reading their Bibles, they begin to relate their life experiences to the ups and downs of these imperfect Biblical characters, and also see themselves in the testimonies of the young people whose stories are shared within the Bible narratives.

"The New Living Translation Bible was easy to read. It was especially helpful that the Bibles we had were student study Bibles. I had tried to read the King James version before, but I could not understand the way it was written. It helped me to have the Bible version written in today's English. It helped me to better understand the message of the Bible, and relate it to my life and what I was going through. The footnote stories about the teens, and the young people placed throughout the Bible really helped me to relate the Bible to my life.

"Once I went to the detention center, I was forced to slow down and reflect on my life. For the first time, I was forced to be away from all the distractions, the cell phone, the drugs. You have to slow down, and you have that Bible with you that Ron gives away to everyone who asks for one in the detention center. That Bible was the only possession that I could keep with me all the time, it was the only thing that I could keep even after I left there, that Bible was mine to keep. That made it even more special to me. I still have that Bible today. With all those distractions gone, and having that Bible written in a more contemporary version, it helped me to understand it and apply what I was reading as I was learning how the Bible applies to my life."

When a young person is living in a detention center, they are separated from everything they know. They are alone with the other inmates and the guards working in the facility, with only the occasional visits from family and friends. It is a place where feelings of loneliness can quickly become an issue for them.

"Having somebody come in who is loving and caring about you, coming to help you is important," stated the young man. "Ron and Doug, they were coming in there on Friday nights, volunteering their time, knowing they are there to work with you. And Ron, he stayed in contact with me once I moved on and he even went to see my family. It was very impactful for me to see what he was doing.

"Once I moved on to the other facility farther away from my home, I anxiously awaited the letters Ron would write to me. From the beginning when I first met Ron and Doug, I could see that they had something that I wanted, something was different about them. When I read Nathan's story in the inside cover of the Bibles, they gave away to us, I realized that this person is sitting here with me who has lost his son, and yet he is here helping me. Ron, he had this peace about him that in the beginning as a new Christian I knew was there, but I could not understand how he was able to do what he was doing, and still have a smile on his face, that peace. That is not something you see every day. Ron is just a regular person like me and knowing that he would come in and give away his time and attention to us, and give away a Bible to anyone who wanted one was amazing.

"Every time he came into the center, he would ask if anyone needed a Bible. He would give a brand-new Bible, still in the plastic wrapper to anyone who wanted one. Those Nathan Project Bibles were all over that facility. The Bibles, they were free to us, but I thought to myself, 'this Bible must be important, there is a reason he wants me to have this Bible,' and that made the Bibles even more special. It told me that this

Bible makes an impact on people's lives, and he wants to share it with me.

"Even at first, I knew there was something different about this person, but I did not know why they were doing what they were doing, but as I began to read the Bible, I would see verses in the Bible that explained to me why they were coming to the center and doing the Bible studies. After reading Nathan's story in the cover of the Bibles, I thought, 'What does Ron have in his life that he can do this work after losing his son?' Ron had this peace in his life that as I read the Bible I began to understand. You would think how can somebody be like this, have this peace after all he has been through. But he doesn't show it?

"When I would read my Bible, I came across verses that would remind me of what Ron was doing, he was living it out. There was one verse in particular that stuck out to me that reminded me of what I saw in Ron. It was John 14, verse 27."

John 14:27 *"I am leaving you with a gift—peace of mind and heart. And the peace I give is a gift the world cannot give. So, don't be troubled or afraid." NLT*

"When I would read this verse, I would immediately think of Ron," recalled the young man, "because he has this peace. And I would think, 'That verse is his life.'

"That's what I saw in Ron, before I could spiritually verbalize it; I saw that peace in the way he lived, that's what you saw in Ron.

"I would 100% credit that being able to turn my life around came from having the Bible and the work that Ron is doing. I started reading my Bible every day and that changed me. It saved me. Ron made it very clear that he would be there for me the whole time.

"I feel that my circumstances happened for a reason. Now that I have been in a situation where someone helped pull me out of a lifestyle that was not good for me, I want to do that same thing, to help pull someone else out of a lifestyle that is hurting them. I had been traveling on a path that I was on, that I could never have gotten out of on my own; there is no way I could have done it, to get off that path alone. I know now, that God let me go through all of that, so that I could see that God could pull me away from that lifestyle.

"Now a major goal for me in my life is to find ways to share my experiences with other people who are in difficult situations in life, because I have been there myself. I know where those roads lead. I was in that spot. I know how deceiving that lifestyle is. I have been in a place where I could only see the short term. Looking back on that time I can see now, that when you are living that lifestyle, Satan is telling you this big lie, and Satan pours that lie into your life. He tells us, 'I have messed up, I've messed up my body, I've burned every bridge and there is no hope.'

"But I can honestly say to someone, with a 100% truthful heart, that no matter where you are in life, there is a silver lining waiting for us in the clouds, when we turn to Jesus and He begins to pull you out of that lifestyle, from the depths of despair, that with Jesus there is always hope."

Conclusion

In the book of Luke chapter 10, verses 25-37, Jesus tells what is in my opinion, the most important short story ever told, because it summarizes what God expects of all of us who choose to follow Christ. The story Jesus tells in this parable, is his response to a question asked him by an expert in religious law, who was attempting to test Jesus.

"Teacher, what should I do to inherit eternal life?" Jesus replied, "What does the law of Moses say? How do you read it?" The man answered, "'You must love the Lord your God with all your heart, all your soul, all your strength, and all your mind.' And, 'Love your neighbor as yourself.'"

"Right!" Jesus told him. "Do this and you will live!"

The man wanted to justify his actions, so he asked Jesus, "And who is my neighbor?"

Jesus replied with a story:

"A Jewish man was traveling from Jerusalem down to Jericho, and he was attacked by bandits. They stripped him of his clothes, beat him up, and left him half dead beside the road. By chance a priest came along. But when he saw the man lying there, he crossed to the other side of the road and passed him by. A Temple assistant walked over and looked at him lying there, but he also passed by on the other side.

"Then a despised Samaritan came along, and when he saw the man, he felt compassion for him. Going over to him, the Samaritan soothed his wounds with olive oil and wine and bandaged them. Then he put the man on his own donkey and took him to an inn, where he took care of him. The next day he handed the innkeeper two silver coins, telling him, 'Take

care of this man. If his bill runs higher than this, I'll pay you the next time I'm here.'

"Now which of these three would you say was a neighbor to the man who was attacked by bandits?" Jesus asked.

The man replied, "The one who showed him mercy."

Then Jesus said, "Yes, now go and do the same." Luke 10:25-37 NLT

* * *

Nathan Stiles was a straight A-student, captain on the football team, a member of the basketball team, and sang in the school chorus. He was a song writer and lead singer of a Christian rock band, and was recognized as Homecoming King of his senior class. But even though he did all of these notable things, what I heard over and over again from everyone who knew Nathan, the thing they remembered most about him, was that he was kind to everyone. It was the way he treated people that mattered most, to the people who knew him best.

It has made a lasting impression on me, that what people told me they remembered most about Nathan, was that he was kind to everyone. His story is a great lesson in the value of kindness. By all accounts, it was his simple acts of kindness, his sharing of God's love, the lessons he learned from his family, his church family, and reading the Bible daily, that molded Nathan into the young man he was.

I never knew Nathan, and I would never say that he, nor any of us for that matter, will attain the level of faithfulness we strive for. Nathan like all of us, could never have achieved perfection, because none of us will ever be perfect.

But the idea that kindness, servanthood, friendship and faithfulness are the qualities we are most remembered for, the attributes that people most remember us by, is a beautiful testimony to what is most important in life. The life we are blessed to live if we choose a life of service and selflessness, the life that Jesus calls us all to endeavor to live out, in his touching story of the Good Samaritan.

Nathan's family has continued this legacy of servanthood and kindness through the Nathan Project Ministry, by gifting away Bibles, many of them to strangers they would never meet, in places they would never go. Since its inception in November of 2010, the Nathan Project has gifted away over 31,000 Bibles.

There is no way to ever measure the many ways these Bibles gifted away by the Nathan Project have affected people for Christ. I have spoken to numerous people myself while working on this book project, who have received a Bible from the Nathan Project and been changed by the transforming power of the Gospel. No one will ever know the long-term impact these people's lives alone, who have been touched by the gift of a Bible, and whose stories are shared in this book, will have on people for Christ throughout their personal ministries for years to come. There is no doubt, that the Nathan Project Ministry and New Living Translation Bibles they have gifted away, are making a difference for Christ today, and will continue to impact people for Christ in generations to come.

And it all began with an act of obedience. When God called Connie and Ron Stiles to action, they showed up. Not knowing for sure where God was calling them to go, they made themselves available.

✳ ✳ ✳

"As time went on our wobbly legs continued on this journey," Ron recalls, "and the Bibles continued to go in all directions. One day, shortly after Nathan had died, as several of us were getting ready to go to a meeting with Pastor Kirk, Connie had Nathan's phone in her hand. She was in need of a newer phone, so she decided to use Nathan's. She looked at his phone and saw that there was a Bible app on it. She decided to look at the last verse saved on his Bible app. It was James 4, starting at verse 13."

'13 Look here, you who say, "Today or tomorrow we are going to a certain town and will stay there a year. We will do business there and make a profit." 14 How do you know what your life will be like tomorrow? Your life is like the morning fog—it's here a little while, then it's gone.' (NLT)

"Once again, my breath was taken away," Ron said. "From that meeting, Pastor Kirk began to write the script that would be the story we put in the Nathan Project Study Bibles that we still use today.

"Not long after that, Pastor Doug approached us about someone he was going to seminary with, that was in need of Bibles. The man he was going to seminary with was Todd Miller. Todd told us that God had called him to minister to the youth in the juvenile center. Todd was leading Bible studies there, and he was in need of Bibles that were easier for the youth to understand. After we met him, he took several cases of the New Living Translation Study Bibles with him, and from there the youth in the facility were on fire for more Bibles.

"Later, Connie and I went to the facility and spoke one day. After speaking in the facility that day Todd asked me to come on a regular basis with him. I told him I did not have the time, and was not sure how well I would do. In the spring of 2011, I decided to go.

"It was a life changing experience," Ron acknowledges.

"I remember there were so many young lives, confused and looking for hope. They all turned into my young friends.

From that we ended up starting another Bible study in a different county. Soon thereafter, the Bibles began to flow into many correctional facilities, not only juvenile but adult as well.

"Our most recent Bible study was started in the adult correctional facility in our local county jail. We have recently built this new facility, and as a county commissioner, I had the honor of being a part of the construction planning for this new jail. In the design process we were able to build a multi-purpose classroom, where they can hold Bible studies and other learning opportunities for the inmates.

"Looking back on it now, who would have ever thought that the day I decided to read the Bible back in 1997, a change would begin in my life that I continue to live today. I remember giving a children's sermon for the first time; I was so nervous I about passed out. Then doing a funeral for a past employee that had a heart attack and died unexpectedly, to now speaking in churches, youth groups and many places I would have never thought I would be. I am thankful for the many friends and supportive people that have been there for me.

"We have all had loss and pain in our lives. Tomorrow on this earth is not certain, but when we have Jesus in our life, we know that tomorrow will never be the end. I will not only miss Nathan, but my other family members and friends that have ended their earthly lives. The message I will continue to share as long as I am able is this; 'Why live for anyone other than Jesus?'"

From the Author

It was an early December morning 2010. I was exercising on an elliptical trainer at a local gym in my hometown of Wilson, North Carolina, when one of the televisions that was suspended from the ceiling in rows facing outward toward the line of ellipticals, treadmills and exercise bikes was tuned to a local ESPN station. As I was moving along through my morning workout, an *Outside the Lines* documentary came on air. It was about a young man from Spring Hill, Kansas, Nathan Stiles.

As I watched the program and heard Nathan's story, the straight A-student, senior captain of the football team, Homecoming King who was kind to everyone and read his Bible every day, who had tragically lost his life after an accident in a high school football game, my heart sank.

I too, at the time, was a parent of high school age children who played high school athletics. I myself had played high school football, and realized that sometimes tragic events happen that none of us can control. As I watched the ESPN documentary that day, I imagined what I would do if I lost my child? How would I respond as a father if it had been one of my children?

Then, as the program continued, there was footage of Ron and Connie Stiles, playing instruments and singing in their church just days after Nathan had died. There was additional documentary footage from a Celebration of Life Service, where days before, Nathan's family announced that there would be a ministry created called The Nathan Project. Their mission was to gift away Bibles to people, to share God's Word with others, so that they, like Nathan, could come to know Christ because that had been Nathan's dream, to lead his friends to Christ.

I remember thinking to myself that day, if they give those Bibles away in response to losing their son, there is no way on Earth that God will not honor such an act of obedience; sharing God's Word, the most important life changing document the world has ever known. Their story was the most touching and amazing act of faith I had ever seen.

Once the program ended and I went home that day, I could not get Nathan's story off my mind. I remember thinking that I should do something to help this family, and this ministry they were beginning. I wanted them to know that I was thinking of them, praying for them, and that I was inspired by their faithfulness and what they were trying to do.

So, I wrote Ron Stiles a letter, and sent them a small donation. Over the next few months, Ron and I spoke over the phone a few times and corresponded on social media. I was in awe of the strength of this amazing family, and continued to be inspired by their selfless acts of faithfulness as they gifted away the Bibles, many going to places they would never have the chance to go, to people they had never met nor would ever meet.

Over the years the Bibles have become seeds, seeds of hope to people in their local community, across the state of Kansas in youth detention centers, and drug rehab centers. Bibles gifted away in prisons across the United States, given away on college campuses, to church youth groups. Given away in YMCA's, given to inner city homeless shelters, missions and churches, and on mission trips to faraway places like Uganda, and various other places taken by people on Christian mission trips around the world.

During these past two years as I have worked on this book project, I have been blessed to meet countless people who have either received a Bible from the Nathan Project Ministry, or who have given away Bibles. Bibles provided to them free of charge, donated by the Nathan Project in support of their ministries. Ministries like Youth for Christ, Christian Challenge Campus Ministry, Fellowship of Christian Athletes, Uganda N.O.W., Kairos Torch Prison Ministry, and countless other churches and individuals who have been impacted in some way through the Nathan Project Ministry.

While working on this project I have learned about so many acts of selflessness, kindness, faithfulness and incredible resiliency, by the people who shared their stories in this book. People who have volunteered their time to work in prison ministry, youth groups, campus ministries, and traveled on mission trips carrying Bibles and the message of hope found in the Gospel of Jesus Christ around the world. I have met multiple families who have suffered the most difficult trial any of us will endure, the loss of a child, and yet in the midst of their pain, they chose to focus on helping others by sharing Christ's love.

I don't know who you are or where you may be as you read this book. Maybe you are reading this book as part of a Sunday school class or a book club, maybe this book was given to you by a coach or youth group advisor. Maybe this book was given to you in a drug rehab center or a youth detention center, or maybe you find yourself in a prison. Or maybe you bought this book in a bookstore, or you are reading it on your phone or computer.

Whatever your situation, wherever you are, know that there is a God who created you, He cares deeply about you. No matter what you may have done, or whatever may have been done to you, know for certain that in this moment, Jesus loves you. He loves you so much, that He chose to go to the cross to save you. He went to the cross for you, and He went there for me. That is a debt that none of us can repay. And if we choose to make Jesus Christ the Lord of our lives, He promises us salvation and grace that none of us can ever earn on our own, no matter how good of a life we live.

Jesus, if you choose to accept His offer of grace and forgiveness, He will walk alongside you in this life, closer than a brother. No matter where you may choose to go, you will never be alone again, because He will be with you always.

If you have not made Jesus Christ the Lord of your life, my hope for you is that you would make the time to find a Bible and read it. And when you read it, read it and study it like a textbook, and as you are reading, pray that God would reveal Himself to you.

When you are able, find yourself a Bible teaching church and go there to visit. Spend time in community with other believers, and seek out God's purpose for your life, as you continue to read your Bible and study the life of Christ.

The reality is, that everyone will make a decision about Jesus. We will either choose to believe He is the Messiah God sent into the world, or we will decide that Jesus is not who He claimed to be. And a choice to make no decision, is a decision to reject Jesus' offer of salvation.

This is the most important decision any of us will ever make.

My hope for you, is that you will invest the time to read and study the Bible and Jesus' life, so that you too can make an informed decision. Then, after that, the choice you make is up to you.

Donnie Prince

Acknowledgements

There have been many people who have given their time and shared their stories with me while writing this book, all of whom have been a great help to me. Getting to know these wonderful people and hearing their stories has been a blessing to me during this process.

I would like to thank, Dr. Wayne Burke, Superintendent of Schools, of the Spring Hill School District, USD 230, and Gary French, Superintendent of Schools, of the Osawatomie School District, USD 367, and their teachers, coaches and staff for their contributions to this book project.

Thank you, to Brian McCauley, Senior Managing Editor, of the Miami County Republic Newspapers, and his staff, for their help and insight into this story, and for sharing their articles and photographs for the book's research with me.

Thank you to the people whose stories and testimonies are shared in detail in the book; Andrew Hudson, Doug Atteberry and Todd Miller, Josh and Michele Ivans, Parker, Shon and Jenny Yust, James, Pat and Susan McGinnis, Travis and Nicole Bosse, Randy Herold and Jose Vega, John and Angie Manning, Bill Corum, Nick Sprague, Jared Brooks, Josie Stiles, Kevin and Rhonda Han, Jim and Linda Hodgson.

Thank you to Nathan's sister, Natalie Stiles Smith, for writing the book's Foreword.

Thank you to Nathan's sister, Josie Stiles, for writing the chapter, Uganda N.O.W.

A very special thank you, to Tom Carbajo, for sharing with me the videos from Nathan's Celebration of Life Service, and the videos of family events that helped me see the story visually as I was writing the book. I am also grateful for his invaluable work, shooting video interviews of people who shared their personal testimonies and spoke of their ministry stories for this book project.

A very special thanks, to Ron and Connie Stiles, for opening their home and sharing their story with me. I have made a whole new set of friends while working on this book project. It has been a great blessing to me to have been allowed by Ron and his family to meet all of these amazing people, who so selflessly are giving of themselves to reach people for Christ.

Donnie Prince

The Nathan Project

If you would like to learn more about the Nathan Project Ministry mission, or if you would like to make a donation in support of their ministry, visit their website at www.nathanproject.com.

ABOUT THE AUTHOR

Donnie Prince is a self-employed business man and author who lives in his home state of North Carolina. He and his wife, Kathy, have two daughters and one awesome grandson. For more information visit his website at play2winlive2serve.com.

Other books written by Donnie Prince:

Play 2 Win Live 2 Serve
The Teacher
An Angel's Journal
Baseball It's More than a Game
Disconnected – The Airius Mission